LECTURES ON MODERN IDEALISM

BY

JOSIAH ROYCE

NEW HAVEN
YALE UNIVERSITY PRESS
LONDON: HUMPHREY MILFORD: OXFORD UNIVERSITY PRESS
MDCCCCXIX

TABLE OF CONTENTS.

THE JAMES WESLEY COOPER
MEMORIAL PUBLICATION FUND

THE present volume is the third work published by the Yale University Press on the James Wesley Cooper Memorial Publication Fund. This Foundation was established March 30, 1918, by a gift to Yale University from Mrs. Ellen H. Cooper in memory of her husband, Rev. James Wesley Cooper, D.D., who was born in New Haven, Connecticut, October 6, 1842, and died in New York City, March 16, 1916. Dr. Cooper was a member of the Class of 1865, Yale College, and for twenty-five years pastor of the South Congregational Church of New Britain, Connecticut. For thirty years he was a corporate member of the American Board of Commissioners for Foreign Missions and from 1885 until the time of his death was a Fellow of Yale University, serving on the Corporation as one of the Successors of the Original Trustees.

EDITOR'S PREFACE.

THE lectures here published were first delivered at the Johns Hopkins University in 1906 under the title "Aspects of Post-Kantian Idealism." They were, in their present form at least, not originally intended for publication, but a note, dated 1907, found among Professor Royce's manuscripts mentions these "Baltimore Lectures" as material "worth publishing." This entitles them to head the list of his posthumous works. Written as they were for oral delivery the lectures required much revision; the editor hopes he has not used his pen too freely.

The subject-matter of these lectures is one that, in a more biographical way, has already been treated in *The Spirit of Modern Philosophy.* The present exposition of post-Kantian idealism, however, is by no means a repetition of the former one. In the earlier book, in which the charm and the depth of Royce's writing reach perhaps their happiest union, the interest is general rather than technical, the tone is popular rather than professional. It contains a rapid survey and not a detailed analysis of the period in question. Yet no other work of his exhibits perhaps in the same degree "the glory of words," the art of vivid phrasing, the gift of graphic and pleasing metaphor, the skill of forcing subtle and difficult ideas into luminous and concrete expression. It is indeed one of the finest feats of Royce's reflective imagination. As a work of deep speculation touched with warm feeling, of historical research cast in original mould, the book has a unique and permanent place in our philosophic literature.

To literary distinction such as the *Spirit of Modern Philosophy* possesses the present lectures can evidently lay no claim. In range and depth, however, they surpass the chronicle of the same period in the earlier volume. There we have but a brief recital of the main phases of post-Kantian doctrine, here an examination of its historical foundation, its logical roots, its human as well as its technical motives. The selection of topics is here more rigorous and the interest more prevailingly theoretical. Moreover, what is here deliberately avoided is the familiar and conventional reproduction of post-Kantian thought. The usual method of the usual textbooks is here not repeated. In vain do we here look for the hackneyed themes of a hundred histories of philosophy. Royce does not seek the successors of Kant in the obvious tracts of ideas. He searches for them in the neglected aspects, the buried documents, the forgotten theses. These reveal to him the true meaning of their teachings; these disclose to him the spirit of the post-Kantian movement. In the early works of Schelling, for instance, Royce finds the pulse of the dialectical method, and in the *Phenomenology* rather than in the *Logic* he discovers the soul of Hegel. And, though the present study is wanting in completeness, there is no shirking of the most difficult problems but rather a choosing of them and a discussion of them with a power, adequacy and clearness which, as we look about, Royce alone seemed able to summon to such a task.

We have particular reason to value at this moment a

dispassionate estimate of that phase of philosophy which, like German music, must suffer through the retrospective judgment of the war. During the present generation it seems difficult to approach without prejudice the products of German genius. The war may be said to have created a "German problem." Shall we condemn and approve uncritically? A double evaluation of Germany seems at first natural enough. Why not condemn her war and her war lords, and admire her philosophy? Unfortunately the boundary between her war and her philosophy is not easy to define. The treacherous onslaught upon the peace of the world in 1914 was no isolated phenomenon. It was the outcome of a definite theory of life.

The hypothesis of continuity in German culture—a culture largely fashioned by technical philosophy—was one which during the war had its protagonists alike among defenders and opponents of Germany. The apologist apologized for all things German; in the eyes of the accuser everything Teutonic appeared tainted. It was not enough to find Germany guilty of this iniquitous war, the guilt must be fixed upon her whole past civilization. Similarly, it was not sufficient to appreciate her past admirable achievements, her deeds in the war must also, since they were German, be the embodiments of the same admirable qualities. The major premise was the same in both cases. Beginning with the assumption of a continuous German civilization, one concluded that it was either continuously bad or continuously good. Germany's past was made responsible for her present crimes; or her present iniquities were cleansed in the stream of her glorious past. Thus it happened that the idealism of Kant, of Fichte, of Hegel became a matter of passionate denunciation or apology. And the books on German philosophy written during the war, instinct as they are with a partisan spirit, can have scarcely more than an ephemeral value.

An unbiased and trustworthy study of German idealism is, therefore, a most notable bequest to the present bewildered generation. It is all the more notable as coming from one who was destined to articulate the American conscience at a time of moral perplexity. He who could with such profound sympathy interpret German thought showed no hesitancy in characterizing Germany as "the wilful and deliberate enemy of the human race" when she, in his opinion, assumed that rôle. Germany was thus judged, not by one who disparaged or belittled, but by one who knew and cherished the ideals of her past. Indeed, this very attitude of sympathy towards German civilization of the past intensified his righteous indignation. The rejection and betrayal of her own ideals constituted for Royce the crime of recent Germany. Because of his deep appreciation of German idealism he was inevitably led to denounce the denial of it by the German state.

The view of the post-Kantian self or Absolute, as interpreted by Royce, throws light on the discrepancy between the earlier idealism and humanism of Germany and her later realism and militarism. The post-Kantian Absolute is no national or tribal deity. "The post-Kantian idealism," Royce summarizes at the close of Lecture II, "was noteworthy in its analysis of the conditions of knowledge. But . . . it was still more noteworthy in its development of social concepts, and in its decidedly fruitful study of the relations which bind the individual self to that unity of selfhood which includes all individuals." *The unity of selfhood which includes all individuals*—this was the post-Kantian ideal; and this ideal of her classic philosophers modern Germany chose to betray. The eternal values which in Kant and his successors possess universal meaning and dignity were cozened by the imperial state into a degrading tribal service. Thus, what one may perhaps venture to call a Social Absolute, universal and supernational in its significance, must be contrasted with the political and national absolutism that dominated latter-day Germany. When and how a spiritual social order, viewed as a universal community, became transformed into a bureaucratic imperial state is a matter of detailed historical study. That Hegel's later doctrines, mutilated and perverted, contributed not a little to the process of Germany's self-estrangement is common knowledge. The merit of Royce's lectures on Hegel consists in replacing the "bureaucratic" tradition which has long occupied the field in discussions of Hegel, both popular and professional, by a more adequate interpretation. The "World-Spirit" of Hegel's philosophy, as Royce shows, is indeed destined to assume, in its "transmigrations," incomplete and defective forms, which must be transcended. That the state, however, in all its phases, from its provincial to its most imperialistic manifestations, is one of the defective forms to be transcended, is Hegel's explicit teaching upon which Royce, in his analysis of the *Phenomenology*, has laid sufficient stress. For the early Hegel the state is an inevitable stage but not the goal of human progress.

The view of the post-Kantian Absolute as a universal community is not without interest for Royce's mental biography. His own doctrine of the community, though on its epistemological side intimately bound up with Peirce's theory of interpretation, is metaphysically not unrelated to the post-Kantian notion of a social Absolute. The social motive is Royce's most characteristic motive. It inspired most of his independent and original thinking. And it is the same motive which accounts in no small measure for his intellectual attachment to the idealism of Kant's successors.

J. LOEWENBERG.

Berkeley, California, July, 1919.

LECTURE I.

KANT'S CONCEPTION OF THE NATURE AND THE CONDITIONS OF KNOWLEDGE.

IN these lectures, I already presuppose some acquaintance with the general history of modern philosophy, and with at least an elementary knowledge of the doctrine of Kant. I wish to offer a partial introduction to the study of post-Kantian idealism. I shall not indeed attempt to tell in any regular order, or to develop in any detail, the history of philosophy since Kant, nor shall I portray any entire period of that philosophy. I shall confine myself to considering selections from the literature of modern idealism, to presenting illustrations of the problems in question, and to indicating how idealism is related to some of the other tendencies of nineteenth-century thought. Even when thus limited, the task is, as we shall see, large enough.

By the term post-Kantian idealism, we name a group of philosophical movements which grew out of the study of Kant's doctrine, and which are, therefore, closely related to it, but which are usually, in one or another respect, opposed to certain of Kant's most characteristic tendencies. These movements form a very varied collection, and cannot be described as the work of any single school of mutually agreeing thinkers. The principal earlier representatives of such idealism, viz., Fichte, Schelling, and Hegel, were already men of highly con-

1

trasted types, and of very marked varieties of opinion. A later representative, Schopenhauer, regarded all three philosophers just mentioned with an aversion whose motives were both doctrinal and personal. Schopenhauer, despite his own form of post-Kantian idealism, laid great stress upon his own hostility to the teachings and to the influence of these his idealistic predecessors. Hegel was, of all the philosophers thus far mentioned, the most successful in organizing a school. But after his death his followers divided themselves into very distinct groups; and to the Hegelian school, in its later developments, have been reckoned men who varied in opinion all the way from the most marked orthodoxy to a pronounced materialism. In more recent times, post-Kantian idealism, influencing thought in France, in England, and in this country, has led to a complication of opinions which it would require many courses of lectures to unravel. A list of those who, with more or less obvious justice, might be called in some sense post-Kantian idealists, would include Cousin, Strauss, Fechner, Lotze, von Hartmann, T. H. Green, Bradley, and even Martineau, despite his pronounced hostility to Hegelianism. And, in a measure, most of our own American pragmatists could be viewed as the outcome of the same movement. Where such varieties of opinion are in question, there is no longer any reason to speak of a school at all. Post-Kantian idealism, viewed in its whole range of manifestation, is not any one theory so much as a tendency, a spirit, a disposition to interpret life and human nature and the world in a certain general way—a tendency, meanwhile, so plastic, so manifold, so lively, as to be capable of appealing to extremely different minds, and of expressing itself in numerous mutually hostile teachings.

2

The expressions of this tendency have, consequently, been of quite as much importance for the history of literature, of social movements, and even of politics, as for the history of technical philosophy. Post-Kantian idealism was prominent among the motives that led Europe into those revolutionary political activities which centered about the year 1848. Since that time post-Kantian idealism has had its part in shaping the great modern conflicts between individualism and socialism. The same general tendency inspired the early growth of our characteristic recent interest in the historical study and appreciation of human institutions; and to the like source must be attributed many of the theoretical motives which have become united since 1860 in the doctrine of evolution. In religion, the idealistic tendency began the large process of reconstruction which within the last seventy years has so transformed both the theology and the practical methods of the non-Roman portion of Christendom. In fact, I think it fairly likely that future historians will look back upon the history of idealism as being that of the dissolution of the classic Protestantism. In literature, post-Kantian idealism has its large share of responsibility for all the varied forms of the romantic movement; and, in a similar way, the same influence has been extended to arts other than literary; so that modern painting and music are not what they would have been without the pervasive effects of idealistic philosophy.

It is worth while then, to try to understand this movement, if only for the sake of its bearing upon the whole course of modern life.

But while I thus point out how broad a field of influence has to be ascribed to post-Kantian idealism, I must at once admit that the field which these lectures will be

3

able to cover is decidedly narrow. For the most part, our study will be confined to matters which belong to decidedly technical philosophy. I shall connect it with an analysis of some of the classic expressions of idealism, but I shall not even attempt a detailed account of the system of any one of the great idealists. In my later lectures especially, I shall try to cover ground which is not usually covered in the textbooks of the history of philosophy, leaving to the student's other training the responsibility for every more systematic view of the history of our period. I shall be selective rather than systematic, illustrative rather than exhaustive. Meanwhile, my task is not with the history of literature, of politics or of religion—closely bound up though the story of modern idealism is with all three of these sorts of human interests—but with some of the central problems of idealism in their more technical aspects. My purpose will be to help you to look at the world, for a time, with the eyes of some one or another of the representative idealists; and to show, by illustrations, why it was that these men viewed things as they did. The early idealists of our post-Kantian period often seem, to the novice, to resemble, according to Hegel's well-known phrase, men who had resolved to try to walk about on their heads. I want to help you to see why these men thought it worth while to view the world in this inverted way. Their exercise of ingenuity may have been somewhat trying to their own endurance and to ours. But their influence was, as I have just pointed out, so manifold and so momentous that it seems worth while to come closer, for a time, to their own point of view, if only for the sake of helping one's general study of nineteenth-century history.

KANT'S CONCEPTION OF KNOWLEDGE

I.

Let me begin our undertaking by calling your attention to that document upon which, as we may forthwith assert, rests the entire process of inquiry which took shape—in the early technically metaphysical theories—of post-Kantian idealism. For while idealism, in its general spirit, was indeed, from the very first, an enormously complicated tendency, due to the revolutionary movement, to individualism, to romanticism, to the whole state of European civilization—just as in turn it reacted upon this whole state of civilization—still, the spirit of philosophical idealism is indeed one thing, its technical expression, in the form of metaphysical doctrines, is another. Had there never been a Kant, there would no doubt have been an idealistic movement in philosophy at the outset of the nineteenth century. But its technical expression would have been very different from that which German idealism received between 1795 and 1830. As matters actually stood, the speculations of Fichte, of Schelling, of Hegel, were worked out under the influence of that formulation of problems which is contained in Kant's writings, and especially in the Kantian *Critique of Pure Reason,* and above all, in the central discussion of that *Critique,* namely, in Kant's famous section called by him *The Transcendental Deduction of the Categories.* Understand the issues stated in Kant's deduction of the categories and you shall understand why these later men formulated their problems as they did; and then you will soon be on the way towards seeing why they proposed the technical solutions which their writings contain. The Kantian deduction of the categories is the portal to the dwelling of modern philosophy. Some of you, having made previous efforts to grasp Kant's meaning,

may regard that portal as a pretty closely shut door—
not only closed, but perhaps locked. And, in fact, the section of Kant's *Critique of Pure Reason* which I have
named is notoriously the most difficult passage in a very
difficult book. But I do not believe the difficulties in question to be insurmountable. In any case, if we are to consider post-Kantian idealism at all, in any of its more
technical aspects, we must make our beginning here, at
the doorway. Otherwise, if we endeavored to avoid such
an entrance to the subject, we should be obliged to view
modern idealism as a passing tourist might view a king's
palace—wholly from without; or, in other terms, our
visit to the dwelling of these modern thinkers would remain, at best, a sort of lawn party. But let us rather
enter the house.

My task requires, therefore, that I shall now try to
portray Kant's main theoretical problem, and the
solution which he proposed for it.

II.

Kant was, in his way, a thinker much devoted to the
reading of the physical sciences as they existed in his
time. He was of course a man of books, not of experi-
ments; but the general theories of science had a large
place in his thoughts. He was especially interested in the
elements of Sir Isaac Newton's physics, in the effort to
conceive the natural world in mechanical terms, and also
in the attempt to distinguish between the fundamental
concepts of the inorganic sciences on the one hand, and of
the organic sciences on the other. His early writings, as is
well known, bear many marks of this fundamental interest in the theories and conceptions of natural science.
He was also a student of metaphysics. Naturally indis-

posed to skepticism, he was still led, by sheer honesty of reflection, to assume, as the years went on, an increasingly critical attitude towards all efforts at metaphysical construction. He was in consequence deeply impressed by one very well-known anomaly of the history of human thought, an anomaly no less obvious in his day than in ours. This anomaly lay in the contrast between the success of the human reason on the one hand, in its efforts both to master mathematical truth and to describe the phenomena that come within the range of natural science, and the failure of the human reason on the other hand, to attain thus far to an agreement amongst the experts regarding the problems of metaphysics. Merely to observe this anomaly is indeed one of the most trivial of commonplaces, and was such in Kant's time. Every scoffer at philosophy delights to point out the contrast in question; and nobody doubts that it exists. But for Kant this contrast was a matter neither for scoffing nor for discouragement. It furnished a problem for what Kant called critical philosophy. Adapting a famous phrase of Spinoza's, we may say that, to Kant's mind, this contrast between the success, both of the empirical sciences and of mathematics, and the failure of metaphysics, was something neither to be wept over, nor to be laughed over, but to be understood. It was precisely his effort to understand why the mathematical and the metaphysical sciences are possible, while the researches of his own and of former times had been doomed to failure—it was this effort, I say, which led Kant to formulate his critical philosophy.

A critical philosophy, in Kant's sense of the term, is neither a constructive metaphysical theory of the ultimate nature of things, nor, like a modern system of Herbert Spencer's type, a summary of the results of physical science. It is, on the contrary, a systematic inquiry into the nature and limits of human knowledge. It is a continuation of the study of the problem which Locke propounded, viz., the problem: What are we men fitted to know?

III.

To this problem, once stated, an answer readily occurs to all our minds—an answer which in our own day has become a commonplace of popular discussion. This answer is, "We are fitted to know what our experience teaches us." This answer to the question regarding the limits of knowledge had been already set forth at length by Locke. The English school of thinkers had repeatedly emphasized its importance; and Hume had been led by the acceptance of this answer to very skeptical conclusions regarding the scope and the limits of our assured knowledge. But whether one viewed the matter skeptically, or felt more cheerful, as most of the partisans of experience always do feel, regarding the wealth and the depth of insight that human experience can give us concerning our world, this answer, "Experience supplies us with all our accessible knowledge," might seem at once to furnish the sufficient reason why the physical sciences had already made, even before Kant's time, such great advances, and why, on the other hand, the metaphysicians whose fortunes Kant had so carefully followed had failed to come to any assured agreement. It would seem, then, that one might try to be contented with saying that physical science had succeeded, as ever since Kant's time it has gone on succeeding, because it investigates and exactly reports what Hume called matters of fact, that is, facts of experience. The metaphysicians had failed, so one might undertake to say, just because they had sought to discover ultimate truth regarding the universe as a whole, about the soul, and about God, while our experience does not present to us the whole world, nor exhibit to us anything ultimate.

Were this all that there is to say about the nature and limits of human knowledge, Kant's work would already have been done for him by Hume. There would be nothing new left for him to say. As a fact, however, while Kant accepted this account of the reason why the natural sciences succeed, and why metaphysical researches had so far failed, as far as this account went, he still could not regard the account itself as, in this form, an adequate expression of what those who accept it have tried to portray. This account was, in Kant's eyes, true but incomplete. It was incomplete for two reasons. It did not adequately analyze what the term experience means. And furthermore, it did not take account of the way in which, side by side and in union with experience, the human reason is able to do profitable work whose results are not mere reports of the facts of experience.

Let us first consider the second of these two senses in which the foregoing account is, for Kant, incomplete. There exist the mathematical sciences. These sciences are the results of certain principles which, as Kant maintained, do not depend upon experience. Arithmetic and geometry, as he always insisted, are therefore not empirical sciences. They deal with what are not, in Hume's sense, matters of fact. Hume himself had asserted in his *Essays* that arithmetic and geometry deal, not indeed directly with matters of fact, but rather with relations of ideas, ideas themselves being, according to Hume, mere shadows, or images, of matters of fact. Kant, however, could not accept this interpretation of the nature of mathematics. For him, the mathematical sciences were a priori constructions. They do not merely report what we find in the world of experience; they determine on the contrary what must be, in the realms of number and of space. Therefore they inevitably arouse afresh the question: Why can the human reason determine a priori what must be in the realms of number and of space—sure that experience can never contradict the demonstration—while nevertheless this same human reason fails to determine what must be in the much more precious realm of metaphysical truth? Both realms would at first sight appear to be capable of exploration by reason, in case either of them is amenable to reason. For if we can get anywhere free from the bondage of experience, why should we not everywhere be free to follow reason into the regions of necessary and a priori truth? If the geometer is able to escape from the duty of merely reporting matters of fact, if he can discover a priori and necessary truth about triangles and circles, why might not the theologian or the philosopher of the soul hope to learn about ultimate truth regarding their topics? Is not the soul of much more value than many triangles?

The difference, then, between the fortunes of the mathematician and those of the metaphysician, needed, for Kant, a special explanation, quite as much as did the difference between the success of the students of natural science and the failure of the philosophers. And mere empiricism appeared to Kant to be inadequate to furnish such an explanation. Hence a new theory of knowledge was, in his opinion, necessary.

And now as to the other inadequacy of Hume's account of human knowledge. It is easy to say that all the truth which we have learned about nature, or about the universe, is empirical truth. Kant, as I have just said, accepted that view. *"Nur in der Erfahrung ist Wahrheit,"* he asserted, in a well-known passage, and in so far he stood beside Hume. But when you have said this you have only begun your theory regarding the true nature of scientific knowledge. Experience is your guide? Granted. But *what* is experience? Is it mere sense impression? No, experience, in a rational being, is a process not merely of receiving sense impressions but of interpreting them. Thought, without the aid of sense, is indeed empty; but sense without the aid of thought is, in Kant's words, blind. Whoever sees without thinking, sees nothing. Therefore you cannot adequately understand what our experience is unless you analyze the part that our nature as thinking beings plays in organizing our experience. If, however, you make such an analysis, you discover, according to Kant, that our experience means something to us solely because we constantly interpret its data in terms of certain ideal constructions or, (in Kant's phraseology,) *schemata* of our own,—schemes due, in their general outline, to the form of our own intelligence. It is the business of a sound theory of knowledge to analyze this form of our intelligence, and to show how its schematic constructions coalesce with our sensations to form our actual and intelligible experience. Hereby we shall prove, according to Kant, that the a priori element in human knowledge, due as it is to the very form of our own intellect, is everywhere exemplified in the unavoidable structure of our experience. No theory of knowledge which fails thus to analyze experience can be adequate to show us why our natural sciences are so successful.

Here, then, lie the two inadequacies of Hume's empiricism, and of all similar views, as Kant understands them: such views *do not show why the mathematical sciences are possible;* and further *do not define what is meant by experience.*

Now Kant maintains that in solving, through his theory of knowledge, the problem, "What is experience?" he has also solved the other problem, "How are the mathematical sciences possible?" The adequate answer to the larger question answers also the other and more elementary one. For, in Kant's opinion, our intelligent experience depends for its entire relational structure upon those forms of our intelligence to which reference has already been made. Of these forms two, namely space and time, are called by Kant the forms of our faculty perception, or in other words, the forms of our sensibility. They characterize us precisely in so far as we are observers of our world, i.e., in so far as we are passive onlookers upon its phenomena. Yet these forms of our perceptive faculty constitute the foundation upon which our active intelligence bases all of its procedure in interpreting the data of our senses. All of our beforementioned constructive schemata, that is, all those ideal outlines of objective structure, in terms of which we interpret the facts of sense, are temporal in their nature. Because of the form of our sensibility, we view whatever is presented to us as a complex of events in time. Furthermore, every form of an outer, or physical event, is also viewed by us, in consequence of the form of our sensibility, as spatial, that is, as a fact that is somewhere in space. And all of this temporal and spatial form of experience is, according to Kant, due, not to anything external to the human mind, but solely to our own nature as knowing beings; and this form of our sensibility is an a priori condition upon which all our experience depends.

Now mathematical science is simply that science which deals with so much of truth as is determined merely by the existence and the nature of these forms of our sensibility. Mathematical science therefore deals, and deals a priori, with the forms or types to which all of our sensible experience must conform. For since these types are a priori, i.e., since they belong to the very conditions of all our experience, and express our own knowing nature, mathematical science has also to be a priori. The things that we are to experience must come to us so as to agree with the forms of our sensibility. Otherwise we should not experience these things at all. But the forms of the sensibility have not, in their turn, to conform themselves to any prior facts of sense experience. The latter may be what you will. Whatever they are, they will have to get into space, or at least into time, or else we, constituted as we are, shall know naught about them. Hence mathematical science, which deals with space and time relations as such, will need no empirical confirmation, and will use none. And yet the very success of mathematical science will be a sort of indirect confirmation of the doctrine, *"Nur in der Erfahrung ist Wahrheit."* For the only reason why we know time and space, geometry and arithmetic, so well, is because the sciences of time and space deal with what the very nature of our knowing self alone determines, namely, the form of our own experience. In order to get a knowledge of the shape of an eggshell you are not, indeed, dependent upon a study of the contents of the egg. And, in a loosely analogous way, for a knowledge of geometrical truth you are not dependent upon a study of physical phenomena as such. But as the only business of an eggshell is to contain the egg, so the only value of time and of space is that they are forms of our human sensibility. We can study them a priori; for they are of our own very life. All study of them is but an analysis of the forms of the knowing self—not an excursion into the realms of absolute reality. Here lies the reason, according to Kant, why the mathematician, who studies in a purely rational way the a priori forms to which all of our experience must conform, succeeds, while the metaphysician, who looks for the road to an absolute reality, fails. So much, then, for mathematical truth.

IV.

One thus sees, in general, that for Kant the great problem of philosophy is the analysis of the conditions upon which all our experience depends. Two assertions characterize his fundamental position with regard to this problem. One is the assertion that the conditions, upon which the form, the structure, the organization of our experience depends, are themselves not empirical, are themselves not facts of sense, are not to be brought to our notice as we learn about single physical phenomena, but are a priori, are for us necessary, are conditions without which we could not conceive or define or find or comprehend any facts whatever, and so are to be discovered through a reflective analysis of our own process of knowledge. The other assertion, so potent for all the development of the later idealism, is this, that when we study these forms of our experience, we are learning nothing whatever about the ultimate nature of anything that exists beyond the knowing self, but are just learning about the self and about its equipment for its life of knowledge. And that, according to Kant, is the reason why any metaphysical knowledge of the ultimate nature of things beyond the self is impossible.

These two assertions of Kant's go very closely bound together. What the moon is, or what yonder remote fixed star is, or what are the laws of physiology—all such things you learn by experience and by experience only. In so far Kant is quite as much an empiricist as is any other student of science. But what experience itself is, so he insists, you cannot learn through mere experience. *That* you must learn by reflection. And reflection concerns itself with the self, for whom, and in whose process of knowledge, the whole realm of experience finds its place. For the remotest star is a phenomenon, a fact in the experience of the self. And the self has its own form of synopsis and of interpretation, in terms of which it sees and thinks all of these facts in whatever unity it discovers them to possess. When you consider however that unity, in which all facts of experience share, only the self can tell you what that unity is to be. The two assertions then: There is knowledge a priori; and such knowledge tells us only about the nature of the knowing self, are closely linked in Kant's mind.

Let us express the matter otherwise: The concept of experience, strange to say, is itself not an empirical concept. An empirical concept is one that you form through observing facts of the sense world. Of a star, of a camel, of a law of nature, you have empirical concepts *only*. You mean, by such facts of nature, facts actually or possibly seen, found, felt, observed, touched, or computed, in accordance with already admitted empirical rules, by some human being, whose intelligence, whose observation and thinking you accept as equivalent to your own. But what human experience is, how it is rendered intelligible, what intelligence is, what it is to observe, to comprehend, to unify facts of experience—all this you cannot learn merely by using your senses, nor yet by intelligently observing phenomena. The knowing self you do not observe as a fact of nature; for it is the observer of all natural facts. You learn of its ways of knowledge through reflection. Your conception of its doings is the conception of the conditions which make experience possible. And this conception is not in its turn derived from experience. It is discovered by finding out the a priori conditions upon which experience depends.

V.

We have formed our first impression of what, according to Kant, the theory of knowledge has to accomplish. We must now consider an aspect of experience which our sketch of the nature of mathematical truth has so far not brought to our direct notice. The physical or empirical facts which we all regard as real are of two sorts. They are, first, the facts which get impressed upon us, from moment to moment, by the present disturbance of our senses. Such are the sounds that now you hear, the walls and the people that now you see. We may call these the facts of present perception. Were you to take all such facts away, and leave us senseless, you would certainly deprive us of all touch with our real world of experience. But, secondly, we constantly deal with facts which are of the type that a contemporary writer, Karl Pearson, (who seems to be very imperfectly aware of how closely he in this respect follows Kant), calls *conceptual constructions*. Let me exemplify: The other side of the moon is a physical phenomenon whose existence we all of us accept; we should unhesitatingly regard it as a fact in the world of

16

experience; yet no man has ever observed the other side of the moon. The interior of the earth is a realm belonging to the physical world. Yet no one has ever extended his direct physical experience further into the interior of the earth than mines and borings have carried us. Countless phenomena, geological, seismographical, astronomical, are indeed interpreted by us so as to appear to throw more or less light upon the physical constitution of the earth's interior. All such interpretations, however, are conceptual constructions which define facts that we view as empirical, while we nevertheless do not even hope to experience them in the way in which we define them. The interior of the earth is very much hotter than any mine or boring has yet directly tested, is under far greater pressure than we have ever observed matter to be—in brief, is a realm of phenomena unlike those with which we are familiar, a realm in which we believe, and believe, furthermore, upon the basis of experienced phenomena, while nevertheless this strange realm of heat and of high pressure refuses to come within the range of live human experience. The stars, the constitution of matter, the geological periods, the process of evolution, the stone age in Europe—these are but a few of the regions of natural fact which come to our scientific knowledge wholly, or principally, in terms of conceptual constructions.

Now I need not here try to describe, with any elaborate detail, in terms of what constructive processes we get individual instances of such conceptions as these. In one sense, experience is our only guide in our efforts to define such conceptual construction. For we get at these constructions, as we say, inductively, upon the basis of what we actually observe. We make hypotheses that are suggested by what we see and find. We confirm or refute these hypotheses by further empirical tests. We regard these conceptual constructions, moreover, as beset with manifold uncertainties, as possessing at best only some higher or lower degree of probability, as being in many ways inferior in their assurance, to the certainty that is possessed by the present facts of experience. Yet, after all is thus said that can be said about the way in which we depend upon present experience as our guide in the formation of these conceptual constructions, the fact remains that, for us all, and at any moment, the natural world "with all its stars and milky ways" is, in the main, precisely a conceptual construction, and is no man's experience. Thus even yesterday's events are already known to you, when you rehearse them in mind, as conceptual constructions. For they are no longer there to be observed. Nor will anybody ever observe them again. Tomorrow's events are also conceptual constructions. Nobody observes them as yet. The things in another room, your home while you are away from it, the contents of any other man's mind, all of these matters are known to you in the form of conceptual constructions. If you ask what truth these conceptual constructions possess, your answer must at any moment be: They possess a truth which I at least do not observe or find as a fact of my experience. And yet, without doubt, you are disposed to view all these facts as of the nature of empirical facts. When is experience not experience? The answer is: When its facts are what most of your acknowledged facts of the realm of experience nearly always are, namely, conceptual constructions.

Without attempting at all to analyze exhaustively the inductive procedure whereby such enlargements of our momentary experience are obtained, I may call attention to two aspects of these conceptual constructions upon which Kant especially insists.

First, in forming these constructions, we not only use, with monotonous regularity, time and space as the general forms in which, as we conceive, all these now unobserved phenomena that we think to be real find their places, but we also employ, with equal monotony, certain *ways of conceiving things,* certain *constructive types,* certain *forms of thought,* which Kant calls *categories.* In terms of these categories we draw the ground-plan, the schema, the outline of possible reality, to which all the objects of our conceived natural world are to conform. We fill out this schema by consulting our actual sense experience. Without some such sense materials, and without images formed after the model of sensory experiences, we should have no means of defining the hypothetical facts that are to fill out this schema. But without categories, that is, general ways of conceiving the structures of things, we should have no schema to fill out. Consider for a moment some of these categories or thought forms. Whatever object we conceive, as for instance the moon or the earth's crust, we conceive as consisting of single, i.e., of more or less elementary parts, the *units* that make it up. Of such units we conceive that pluralities, complexes, or assemblages exist. These complexes in sufficient number form *systems,* such as an organism, or a planet, or a solar system exemplify. Such systems possess a certain rounded *totality.* Thus *unity, plurality, totality* are three forms in terms of which we conceive all our objective world. Kant himself supposes that our ideas of the measurable quantities of the physical world are due to these thought forms. Or again, if we conceive, as we always do, a world of changing objects, we conceive that all physical

19

changes leave invariant certain material substances whose nature we can only define in terms of our actual experience, but whose existence we conceive whether present experience enables us to fill out the scheme or not. To take an instance from recent experience, if radium proves to be transformed as it changes into some other material phenomenon, say helium, then we tend to assume at once that these changes have occurred to something that lies beneath the changes in question, and that, bĕing itself neither mere radium nor mere helium, remains invariant through the change. *Something is invariant, wherever change occurs*—this presupposition defines for us, according to Kant, a schema, in terms of which all observed changes are to be interpreted. And this schema expresses a type of thinking, a category, characteristic of our intelligence. This is the category of *Substance*. In a similar fashion we conceive events as always being instances of invariant rules, the laws of nature. What these laws are, experience alone can tell us. But *that there are laws,* invariant from event to event, and omnipresent, this is a principle in terms of which all of our conceptual constructions are made, however well or ill we may as yet have learned from experience what the laws of nature are. This schema, this outline plan of things, in terms of which we build up the whole world of conceptual constructions, is due to a type of thinking which Kant calls the category of *Causation*.

The result of our possessing such categories is that we carry about with us a sort of outline plan of the natural universe. We fill in this scheme solely by means of experiences, and of images derived from experience. But the plan itself is a priori, and is, for us, necessary. Without categories, no conceptual constructions. Without a general outline of the form of reality, no means of defining tests for distinguishing real from purely fanciful constructions. Without conceptual constructions, however, we should possess no acknowledgment or recognition of past or of future, no acceptance of the now unseen natural phenomena, no conspectus of any physical realm whatever—nothing but the dream of an incomprehensible present. It follows, thinks Kant, that it is the form of our own intelligence which determines the intelligible structure of the whole natural world that we acknowledge as real. So much for the first of the two aspects of the conceptual constructions here in question.

The second aspect is closely bound up with the first. I do not merely conceive of the phenomena that are not now visible to me; I also conceive them all as linked into some definable unity which connects them with my present experience. For what is now happening to me I view as merely an instance of a process of experience which virtually or possibly includes all physical facts. And all of the other facts of experience which I acknowledge, but which are now conceptual constructions to me, I view as possible experiences of mine, and therefore as possessing an unity which is the correlate of the unity of my own self. I also view these same facts as possible experiences of yours or of any other human being; for I regard all human experiences as belonging to a single system, to a single unity of possible experience. There is then, says Kant, virtually but one experience. And all physical facts are conceived as facts existent for this one experience, and thus as mutually linked. We conceive all momentary observations of ours as fragmentary glimpses of that one experience. The unity of the physical world is therefore conceived by us in terms of the unity of a sort of ideal or virtual self, the self of an ideal or possible human observer of whom we conceive that whatever fact we acknowledge to be real in the physical world is ipso facto viewed as observable by this self. This ideal or virtual self is, for any one of us, myself, my larger unity of experience. When I think of you as experiencing the same physical world that I experience, I do so because I then conceive our experiences as being virtually the experiences of a single self, that is, as being subject to the same categories, and as united in a common process of knowledge. Whatever fact of nature I conceive as real, I thus conceive as a phenomenon for that virtual self, whose experiences I from moment to moment exemplify, whose categories I from moment to moment employ, and whose unity of possible experience is correlative with whatever unity I ascribe to the natural world.

Kant nowhere says, and certainly nowhere intends, that this self to whose categories all natural facts conform has anything but a virtual, a conceived, unity of consciousness. He nowhere means that this self should be viewed as any absolute, or as any superhuman mind that views all the facts of nature at once. He is speaking only of human intelligence, and only of how we men have to view, that is, to conceive and to experience our facts of nature. What he holds is that those facts of nature which we conceive, but do not observe, have (1) to be conceived by us in accordance with our categories, or forms of thought, and then (2) have to be conceived by us as possible objects of our own experience. In order thus to be viewed, these now unseen facts of nature have to be conceived by us as so related to what we do now experience that this very relation itself is also the possible object of our own experience. Thus all natural facts are conceived as present to a single virtual unity of consciousness, the virtual unity of the consciousness of the self. This self one inevitably conceives as common to all those men whose intelligence we accept as essentially a guide to our own.

VI.

I suppose that one may have listened to all the preceding discourse, and may still be disposed to reply to Kant somewhat as follows: This account seems, so far as stated, to be wholly an account of how we men find it convenient to conceive things. But man's true scientific interest is in things as they are and not in his private conceptions. Now from moment to moment, whatever our categories may be, experience comes to us in its own way, and independently of our will. And however we may conceptually construct the now unseen world, that world actually contains whatever it contains, and again independently of our will or of our way of thinking. What a priori guarantee is there then that these our ways of conceiving things are well warranted? Why might not the genuine natural world simply ignore our categories? If it did so, and experience failed to confirm our ways of conceiving things, what could we do to enforce our conceptional constructions? Present experience, in any case, is not a mere conceptual construction. Why might not the unintelligible happen? Why might not experience break away from the forms of my intellect? Why might not chaos come at any moment? That such chaos does not now occur, what is that but itself a merely empirical fact, neither a priori nor necessary?

To answer just such questions, so far as the categories were concerned, was the purpose of Kant's so-called

23

deduction of the categories. This deduction is an effort to prove, not only that we are subjectively forced to conceive all facts as being in accordance with the forms of our intellect, but also that we can be sure that the objective facts of what we call nature actually never will transgress the limits which our intellect sets when it defines the foregoing outline plan of our world.

Kant's deduction may be summarized in our own way as follows: We men never deal or can deal with any facts which are totally independent of our nature. We never deal with things as they might exist in and by themselves, in case there were nobody there to know them. On the contrary, we deal with phenomena, with facts as they appear to us. It is then not surprising that our nature as knowing beings should have a great deal to do a priori with the way in which what we call facts should be constituted. Our physical world is, after all, the world as we see it and as we conceive it, and is therefore simply not independent of our nature. It is, on the contrary, a human world—a world that men find and think and define and verify. What wonder then if it actually conforms to our necessary and human point of view? If it did not, how should we ever come to know the fact that it did not? For such knowledge would be knowledge, and so far would have to conform to the conditions which make our knowledge possible.

But these are generalities. Let us come still closer to the precise situation by showing how experience from moment to moment gets its structure. I see just now these facts before me. I see this room, these walls, these people. But intelligent seeing is not mere acceptance of data. It is a more or less spontaneous response to things. It is a doing as well as a viewing; it is intelligent as well as

24

receptive; it is constructive as well as submissive. I look at things. That means: I move my eyes, I turn my head, I reconstruct the contours of the objects upon which my gaze fixes itself. My observation is a mode of living, a fashion of behavior, a stamping myself upon my world. For after all, I from moment to moment see in things what I am prepared to think into things. Experience is a synthesis of contents, a weaving together of data, a process of building up the connections of things. And in all this active process of experience, am I not at every instant expressing myself as well as reflecting any foreign nature of things?

Well, even when I thus actively experience the presence of what is independent of my will, I still of course use, from moment to moment, my categories. It is not surprising that whatever I actually observe and make the topic of assertions has to conform to my essential modes of observation and of judgment, and that whatever I am to understand must be, in its outline structure, such as to lend itself to the demands of my understanding. So far, a deduction of the applicability of my categories to whatever facts are to come under my notice, appears identical with the observation that facts cannot at any moment be forced upon me in such wise as to become intelligible to me at all, without the active coöperation of my own intelligence. So, therefore, whatever I am at present to understand must always be such as conforms to the type of my understanding. If quantity and quality, if unity and plurality, if the sharp outlines and clear limitations of things, if conceived permanence of objects, and if conformity to some sort of laws regarding the sequence of things—if all these are ideas in terms of which I necessarily must interpret the facts of sense which are now before me, unless I am to fail intelligently to grasp these facts at all, then indeed it seems fair enough to say that from moment to moment only the relatively coherent experience is fitted to survive for my attention, as any experience of facts at all. Attention then always secures a sort of survival of the fittest amongst my experiences. I can intelligently note only what is fit to be known, the more or less orderly and not the merely chaotic.

Now all this indeed seems to throw light upon the present conditions to which my experience must conform if I am just now to view that experience as in any way for me intelligible and significant. But, as you may still insist, does this throw any light upon what sorts of facts and laws the whole wide range of infinite nature must contain? The distant stars, the interior of the earth, the constitution of matter, the evolution of species—do I thus know anything a priori about even the outline structure of these so distant and manifold facts? The nature of things is whatever it is. I did not make the world. "Where wast thou when I laid the foundations of things?" So the Lord of the whirlwind might say to me as to Job. What power have my categories over such a Lord, or over whatever power it is to which the natural world is due?

Kant replies, in substance, by insisting that when you talk of nature and of the great whole of things you must mean something by what you talk about. If you speak of a natural fact, you cannot speak of things as they would be in case nobody knew them, or as they are in case nobody knows them. You must speak either of what you now observe or else of what you conceive as observable by you. Facts of any other sorts than these are simply indefinable by you and are unknowable. Or again, you must so think of facts as to define them with reference to the conditions of your possible experience. Else are they no facts for you at all. Your world, in other words, consists either of what you see or of what you think. And what you think, if your thought has any sense at all, is conceived in terms of some experience that, as you suppose, you might have. Define, however, any of your possible experiences. Where must you inevitably place it, in order to give any meaning to your definition? Kant answers, "In the same totality of conceived experience as that in which you place the very fact which you now see." For all your possible experience has to be conceived by you as linked by definable ties to your present experience. Else you do not conceive such possible experience as yours at all. And these links have to be so conceived by you that you can at least regard yourself as virtually authorized, by your relation to the world, to take all the facts whose reality you can acknowledge into the single unity of one view. You can then at least conceive yourself as saying to all facts, "Yes, these are facts, for I, the one self, experience them." Unless you at least conceive such an unity of view as possible, you do not define the facts of your world as, for you, genuine facts at all. Only of such phenomena can you speak. With things in themselves you have, in your knowledge, nothing whatever to do.

Hence, as Kant insists, in acknowledging facts as real, you have to view such facts as determined in their nature by the very conditions which make the unity of your present experience possible. Whatever object is now before you, and is observed and noted by you, plainly has a structure whose outlines your own nature as an intelligent user of your categories determines. And, even so, whatever object is *not* now before you, it is still conceived as a real or as a possible fact of nature, is conceived as *virtually* yours to observe, to define and report, to connect with the present and with all other facts into a single united whole of experiences. Nature is real for you in so far as you can conceive that were it not for your empirical limitations of consciousness you could observe all its facts at one glance. Hence, all natural facts, whatever they are, must be viewed by you as if an intelligence, virtually identical with your own, determined, not indeed their empirical details, but their general outlines in conformity with the laws of your intelligence, constructed them as if to exemplify your categories, drew them, so to speak, as a geometer draws lines, put into them that intelligible structure which you now think into present facts. As we have already pointed out, this virtual intelligence, to whose categories whatever facts you are to regard as real must conform, is indeed not, for Kant, any concrete or absolute or divine intelligence at all, but is simply that presupposed virtual unity of consciousness in conformity with whose categories you have to think facts in order to conceive them real at all. For if what I now note has to conform to the laws of my intelligence in order to become notable, what I conceive as real has still to be conceived as possibly observable, not only in its own structure but in those relations which bind it, with all other real facts, into the unity of a single conceivable and possible observation.

Let us briefly sum up this whole lengthy survey. It is indeed true, according to Kant, that our knowledge is limited to facts of experience. But it is also true that we know a priori, and in outline, what the structure of these facts must be. In so far as this structure is simply one of time and space we can define it a priori by means of a mathematical science of those forms of all our observation which are called time and space. Such a science is not empirical, and yet is possible only because it predetermines what the mathematical forms of all empirical objects must be. Similarly, there is a further science a priori of the formal outline structure to which all physical objects and relations and laws of objects must conform. This science of the very conditions which every definable object of common sense and of our natural science must illustrate, tells us in advance, not what facts we shall find, but what sort of unity all experience must possess in order to be conceived as our possible experience in any sense whatever. These conditions of the unity of possible experience are our categories, our ways of conceiving and of describing things. We conceive them as the laws in accordance with which a certain conceived self, identical in its intelligent nature with our own intellect, virtually constructs for us all natural facts out of the raw material which sense from moment to moment presents. This virtual self, and its understanding, we must conceive as the source of the types to which all natural laws and facts must conform.

Such, in summary, is Kant's deduction of the categories, his attempted proof that all natural facts must conform a priori to the conditions which our intelligence determines. Essential features of his attempted proof are (1) the assertion that all natural facts are phenomena, not things as they would or might be in case nobody knew them; and (2) his view that all phenomena, as possible objects of experience, must conform to the laws of the possible unity of consciousness of a single self whose complete experience we never attain but are always seeking, and whose nature we conceive as virtually identical with the very intelligence that from moment to moment gives order to our passing experience.

LECTURE II.

THE MODIFICATION OF KANT'S CONCEPTION OF THE SELF.

I POINTED out in beginning the last lecture that the present course can undertake no connected history of the idealistic movement, but is limited to a sketch of some of its principal conceptions and to illustrations of its manner of thinking. You will therefore not demand of me any detailed account of the steps that led from the first philosophical discussions which took place after Kant published his *Critique of Pure Reason* to the time when the post-Kantian idealistic movement was in full swing. In our first lecture I gave an outline of the main thoughts of Kant's deduction of the categories. I asserted that out of these thoughts the principal considerations which the later idealism emphasized may be said to have developed. My present task is to indicate, in the most general way, how this development took place. But I shall not attempt to portray the annals of philosophical thought in the closing years of the eighteenth century.

I.

Kant's deduction of the categories, as we saw, made prominent what we may now restate as four distinct but closely related thoughts. The first of these has become a commonplace of all modern philosophy. It is the thought that we do not know things as they are or as they might be in themselves, that is, apart from knowledge, but we know only phenomena, that is, things as they appear to us. In stating this thought, Kant made especially prominent one aspect of it, namely the view that all facts which can be known to us are facts determined in their general and necessary types by whatever mental conditions make knowledge possible for us. We can never know what the facts would be apart from the occurrence of knowledge itself; we can only know facts as the process of knowledge not only colors but actually defines and determines their appearance. The mind sees itself in all it sees. There is no way of telling what the world would be were there no intelligence to observe it. The world that we know is the world that our intelligence observes; and the nature of the intelligence is, therefore, an essential factor in the constitution of phenomena.

The second thought which Kant's deduction makes prominent is the thesis that we can know, not only in general but in detail, through reflection, just *what* these necessary and universal conditions are upon which our knowledge itself depends. For these conditions are no mystery, such as would be the things in themselves, but are due to our own intelligence, whose workings we have a right to know. These conditions, in fact, constitute what Kant calls the form of our known world. They are time, space, and the categories of our understanding. These as conditions of our knowledge predetermine the outline structure of our known universe. You do not know what physical things there are on the other side of the moon. But you are sure that there is space there and that space has in the lunar regions the same geometrical characters as the space in this room. You do not know precisely what events occurred in prehistoric times. But you are confident that time itself had then the same formal characters as now. The geometrical and the temporal outlines of all parts of your world is, thus, predetermined by the form of your consciousness of time and of space. Furthermore, in Kant's opinion, you define, in certain outline schemes, that structure of the world, as a system of units and of complexes, of quantities and of qualities, of substances and of laws—that structure which, according to him, the categories of your intellect predetermine. You do so although you cannot predetermine how this outline structure is to be filled out, but must leave to experience to show what units, what complexes, what quantities and qualities, what substances and laws, nature is to present to you. Space, time, and the categories, are thus, according to Kant, the a priori aspects of knowledge. This does not mean that they are innate ideas, such as Locke assailed, and such as should belong to the psychological furniture of the mind at birth. What Kant means is simply that space, time, and the categories are the forms *logically* characteristic of our intelligence whenever and however it develops, so that if we did not interpret facts in terms of these forms, we should simply have no human intelligence whatever, but should be beings of some other type, whose states of mind, whatever else they then might be, would at least not be human thoughts. When Kant calls these forms of our intelligence a priori forms, he means simply that every act of our mature intelligence must make use of these forms in defining the outline sketch or scheme of that world in which we find all our facts. His view is that a fact is a fact for us only in case it can take its place somewhere in such a scheme as our intelligence outlines a priori.

The third thought which Kant's deduction emphasizes is the thought that these a priori forms are of no use to us whatever except in so far as we employ the data of experience to fill out the forms. My outline scheme of my world is indeed indispensable to me; and the word *a priori* in so far means for Kant simply the same as *indispensable*. But this outline is meaningless unless it gets a filling. The form is vain without the matter. And the form cannot furnish its own matter, cannot fill out its own outlines. It is my experience which gives me the matter. My forms never tell me of themselves the material facts that the senses are to show. Thus, for example, every physical phenomenon must be in space, and so must conform to the laws of geometry. That is, for Kant, an a priori truth. But geometry cannot tell me anything about what physical facts are in space. That is to be learned only by experience. Kant's principle then is that the forms of the intelligence are nothing but the formal conditions of our possible experience. And that again is precisely why they tell us nothing about any truth regarding a world beyond experience. Our knowledge is not enlarged by the a priori forms beyond the range of experience. We know through them only the conditions which are indispensable in case experience is to be obtained, held fast, described, and rendered intelligible.

The fourth characteristic thought in the deduction is the thought that we conceive all our experience as unified, as connected, as interrelated, in so far as we view the whole realm of knowable facts as the experience of one virtual self whose time and space forms, whose categories, whose data of knowledge, whose possible experiences, form the topic with which all our sciences are busied. This self we view as one, although we can never find out the ultimate basis of its unity or its deeper nature. We attribute intelligence to other men only by viewing their selves as, for purposes of mutual comprehension, one, in intelligent selfhood, with our own self. The knowable world is the realm of the possible experience of this virtual self to whose *one* experience we inevitably refer any natural fact. This one self is indeed, for Kant, as we saw, not a knowable metaphysical entity, but merely a formal presupposition of the theory of knowledge. To say, "This is a fact in the world," is to say, "This I view as, under definite conditions, a possible experience of mine." To say, "Other men know the same physical facts that I know," is to say, "I accept other men's experience as virtually in the same unity of experience in which I myself am." To say, "Facts are subject to the forms of intelligence, to the categories, to time, to space," is to say, "These forms are the forms of the experience of the self. All experiences are parts of this conceived single experience. These forms are the forms of the intelligence of the self."

This is Kant's conception of the nature and the conditions of knowledge.

II.

Now it is easy to see that such a view is in somewhat unstable equilibrium. It is a marvelous synthesis of motives which most men find very conflicting. I have tried, in my brief exposition, to be as just to these motives as the case permits. But my very statement must arouse a feeling to which Kant's contemporaries gave frequent expression. This feeling is essentially this, that in order to get into the realm of Kant's theory of knowledge—in order to view facts and to define truth as he did—you have to admit conceptions which, in their turn, seem to render it impossible to remain permanently in that realm when once you have got in. Kant had a very singular power of holding his judgment suspended regarding matters that almost any disciple of Kant is at once tempted to decide, and to decide in a way that leads to a modification of the Kantian doctrines. Kant was curiously able to regard as unanswerable certain questions which almost any man who even temporarily assumes a Kantian position insists upon asking, and is almost certain to attempt an answer. You may or you may not in the end come to agree with Kant. In any case it is easy to understand the temptations by which his disciples and his critics were moved when they proceeded to modify what they had learned from him as soon as they had learned it. Let us consider a little some of these elements of instability which a closer consideration shows to exist in the Kantian doctrine.

The first point which here meets our notice is the famous problem regarding the "things in themselves."

We know, said Kant, only phenomena, only things as they appear to beings whose unity of experience, whose forms of intelligence, are ours. We do not know things as they are when nobody, or nobody like ourselves, knows them. One may at once reply to Kant, "What do you mean, then, by your things in themselves, which are, but are unknowable? Do you mean merely to suggest the bare possibility, the purely abstract hypothesis, that, apart from all human knowledge, there might be an object or a world of objects, that nobody such as we mortals are knew or could know? Do you merely mean to say that *if* there be, or *if* there were, any such things in themselves, we, who know only in our own way, and according to our own lights, could not find such facts amongst our

36

phenomena? Or, on the other hand, do you mean directly to assert that there *are* things in themselves—a world of indubitable facts existent apart from all human knowledge, a supersensuous realm, a beyond—and that we mortals have no access to that realm, being confined to mere phenomena.''

Kant unquestionably meant to hold the second of these two views. To his mind there was never a doubt that, quite apart from human knowledge, there is an absolutely real world to which we can apply the name ''the world of things in themselves.'' To this world, in fact, even we ourselves belong, according to Kant, in so far as our own selves have some basis, to us at present unknowable, some root grounded in the nature of things outside of our own present conscious knowledge, but real nevertheless in a sense in which no phenomenon, mental or physical, is ever real. Even our own personal consciousness never shows us what we ourselves are. Yet *that* we are is indubitable. Our true self is thus not our conscious self. Beneath the phenomena of our inner life, beneath our feelings, our thoughts, our phenomenal character, our apparent motives, there is the real man, the self of the self, the heart of hearts within us, or rather, as Kant would prefer to say, the genuine will that in each one of us is only phenomenally indicated by what he seems to be doing in the phenomenal world. Kant held this view, in case of the self of each one of us, for reasons which he could not articulate in purely theoretical terms, but which his ethical philosophy, developed in his later work called the *Critique of Practical Reason,* made especially prominent. Observe the phenomena of your inner life. They come and go like other matters of experience. Looking at them theoretically, you can define their form a priori, somewhat as you can define the outline form of other phenomena. Unlike other phenomena, those of the mind are viewed by you as taking place simply in time, and not, like material phenomena, as also occupying space. But you view these mental phenomena as facts subject to the types of law which your categories determine. If you study psychology, you try to reduce the mental phenomena to an intelligible system of facts of experience, just as you treat other phenomena. In this way you learn, not what you really are, but how you seem to yourself to be. But when you act, when you choose something, you nevertheless have a certain practical faith which you express by saying, "I did this deed; nobody else did it. I am the true source of this deed, which originated nowhere else." *This* faith is, according to Kant, incapable of any psychological verification by any study of mental phenomena. If you observe your inner states, you can only note a certain sequence of experiences, of feelings, of interests, of images, and a certain relation between these states and the outer phenomena, the movements of your body. You cannot see where your mental states come from. As psychologist you are interested merely in attempting to connect these states of yours with other phenomena, according to laws which exemplify the categories of your understanding. But no such discovery of how your mental states are psychologically caused is ever just to the demand of what Kant calls your practical reason. For the practical reason says, "I am the author of my own deeds." Now, in your inner life, you never observe this author of your deeds. There is nothing in the realm of mental phenomena that appears, or that can appear to be the first author, the actual doer, or originator of anything whatever. The inner life shows you only states of mind which your understanding views as the result of various antecedent phenomenal causes; and this chain of antecedents you are obliged to extend backwards indefinitely, without ever being able to conceive its temporal or phenomenal origin. None the less, the practical reason, in passing moral judgments, inevitably says, "I am, for I ought to be, the origin, the source of my own deeds." And the faith thus asserted is, for Kant, rationally as unconquerable as it is, for us, unverifiable. This is the faith which Kant defines, in his *Critique of Practical Reason,* as the postulate of the freedom of the will.

Since the phenomenal or empirical self of the inner life, the "me," is thus viewed by our understanding as an effect of conditions, never as an originator of anything, while the moral consciousness inevitably, and, as Kant holds, rightly, believes that I am in very truth the initiator of my deeds, it follows, according to Kant, that the true self is no phenomenon of the inner life, is not presented to our observant consciousness, but has a reality of which we are not now conscious at all, a character which no phenomenal heredity and no gradual formation of observable habits can determine, a nature which no introspection reveals. This true self is no fact in space or in time. It is subject to none of the categories of our understanding. It is to us unknowable, but indubitable—undiscoverable in inner experience, but responsible for all our activity. It is our ethical postulate, but not our verifiable datum. It is not the psychological "me," but the ethical "I."

To sum up: This doctrine, which Kant develops at length in his ethics, has an essentially practical basis. We cannot consciously observe our own real nature. But we act as if we had one, for which we are ethically responsible. And we ought so to act. In his ethics Kant is guided by what, in his opinion, is a perfectly rational faith that each of us possesses, or rather is, a true ego, now out of our own range of observation, but absolutely real; the phenomena of the inner life are only the shadow, so to speak, of this true ego, the mere hint that it gives to the understanding of how it displays and hides itself.

Now just as Kant thus feels sure of a true ego, which is no phenomenon of consciousness, but which is the true author of our deeds, the very life of our will, he likewise finds indubitable, although never phenomenally verifiable, the view that behind all external phenomena there are genuine things in themselves, as unknown to our intellect as they are impenetrable to our senses. Yet without these things in themselves, as Kant holds, our senses would have no contents to present to our thought, and our thought no phenomena to conceive in accordance with the categories of the understanding. The things in themselves being other than the true ego somehow affect our true ego. The result is first that our senses are impressed by certain data, and then that the understanding is aroused to apply its forms to the intelligent conception of these data. As a consequence, we come to see the phenomena before us and to view physical objects as real. The physical objects are indeed only phenomena. The phenomena are the show of an otherwise unknowable yet absolutely real world.

So far Kant's view of the ''things in themselves,''—a doctrine partly inarticulate and partly ethical, at once the deepest and the least satisfactory of his personal presuppositions in philosophy.

KANT'S CONCEPTION OF THE SELF
III.

Kant's followers and critics have nearly always found this view, as I said before, unstable. It is one thing to say: We know things as they appear to us. It is another thing to say: We know that there are absolutely real things which nevertheless do *not* appear to us, and which never can appear to us. The inevitable question arises: How are we able to know so much, and yet so little about these things in themselves? So much; for although they never appear in our experience, and although we never verify their presence, as we verify phenomenal facts, we yet somehow know *that* they are. So little; for although we thus know that they are, we can never, by any possibility, learn *what* they are, so long as we are in this present form of life, and are possessed of any human type of knowledge whatever.

This question, once raised, refuses to be answered without a revision of the Kantian concept of the things in themselves. The simplest revision would seem to be one which had some part in forming the views of the post-Kantian idealists. This simplest revision would involve a mere dropping of this concept, as a paradoxical one, incapable of definite articulation. If knowledge is of phenomena, why talk of any world but the world of phenomena? If all the sciences are concerned simply with the laws of phenomena, why pretend to acknowledge the existence of things in themselves, beyond all possible knowledge? To be sure, both science and common sense intend to deal with a real world and not with a world of fantasies or of merely present mental states. But then Kant's world of phenomena is not an unreal world, nor is it a world merely of present sense perception. It is a world of orderly possibilities of experience. Its facts and

41

laws are valid for every man, and are capable of being tested in definite ways by processes which involve turning possible experiences into actually present experiences. A visible fixed star is indeed a phenomenon. It is not on that account something which, for Kant, is subjective. It is an objective phenomenon, for all astronomers can observe it, and can define its apparent place by the same astronomical coördinates and can verify the definition. We eat and drink, we buy and sell, we wear and we store up in our houses, not things in themselves, but phenomena. Yet Kant holds, like any common sense man, that all these phenomena are objective, and are in no wise phantasms. What makes them objective is that they are subject to definite empirical laws. Kant has shown, as he thinks, *why* these laws hold for phenomena. His deduction of the categories was concerned with that problem. In any case, whether you accept Kant's deduction or not, the phenomena are the facts about our world which alone interest our science. Hence one may well ask what good the things in themselves are to anybody, since one can neither investigate, nor possess, nor consume, nor even define them.

Nevertheless the case of the true self, the free agent, of Kant's ethical doctrine, still gives us a little pause as we try to make up our minds about the fate of the things in themselves. Whether you accept Kant's view of the self or not, there can be no doubt that his practical teaching concerning that self which I am to view as the author of my own deeds has its own special interest. The fact that no psychological analysis ever discovers the first origin of any mental phenomenon whatever, while I yet have a deep and morally significant tendency to ascribe to myself an originative character as the source of my own

42

deeds—all this, I say, furnishes a motive for speaking of the true self as no phenomenon, and as at once beyond and beneath all my present consciousness. This motive the principal post-Kantian idealists, as we shall soon see, fully appreciated. It suggests rather a modification than a simple dropping of the conception of things in themselves. What such a modification might involve is further suggested by an aspect of phenomena which both Kant and common sense recognize, and which was pointed out in our previous lecture when we were sketching Kant's deduction.

We deal with the phenomenal world, and the laws of our own intelligence determine the outline structure which its facts must possess in case they are to take any place at all in our sciences or in our lives. But as we saw, this outline structure is not its own filling. The form of things, according to Kant, we know a priori, but the form does not, to our view, determine the matter. In other words, we are conscious of phenomena; and, according to Kant, we can become conscious a priori of the types of law which phenomena must exemplify. We are not conscious of the source of our experience. We are not conscious of why just these facts must be presented to our senses. We have passively to await the verdict of experience regarding what data are to fill out our intelligent outline plan of things.

This being the case, it is natural to say that since phenomena, although, in Kant's view, objective, are still facts for a possible human consciousness, while human consciousness is an expression of the self, therefore the source of our experience may lie hidden in that very nature of the real self which Kant, in his ethics, postulates as the source of our deeds. The true self is hidden from us. It is no phenomenon. Yet it is that which actually does our deeds. May it not in some way originate our experience also? May not its hidden nature be responsible for the matter of experience as well as for the form? May not the self be the only true thing in itself? May not sense and understanding both spring from a common to us unknown root? In a famous passage Kant himself had suggested, in a purely problematic sense, this very possibility. The early post-Kantian idealists agreed in an endeavor to frame such an hypothesis, and so far as might be, to develop and to verify it.

Things in themselves seemed to us, a moment since, useless, because only phenomena are definable in terms of human knowledge. Now we see two motives that might tend to modify this general verdict. The first motive is furnished by the self. In the case of the self there exists a problematic union of observable mental phenomena with a practically significant assertion of its own ethical significance on the part of the self—a problematic union of "I seem to be thus or thus in my mental state" with "I will do this or this." This union of the phenomenal and the significant, of the mere sequence of states and the originative will, suggests that we are deeper than we seem to be. We are more than merely phenomenal. The second motive lies in the fact that while the phenomena, although objective, are still our own experience, and thus partake of the nature of the self, they still seem such that we are not now conscious why they belong to the self. We are not now conscious why we experience what we do experience. This suggests the possibility that the experience of the self has, like our own deeds, a source in the now hidden nature of the self.

Both these motives proved potent with the post-Kant-

ian idealism. How potent, and with how reasonable a
result, we shall later see.

IV.

We have now seen one instability of Kant's view regarding knowledge, and have defined one tendency that
led later thinkers to modify his view. Herewith the case
for a modification of Kant's views is not closed. Kant
undertook to define with precision the a priori forms in
terms of which our intelligence finds its own in the phenomena. The question very naturally arises: How did
he find out what these forms are? His list of them is
made up, indeed, of familiar names: time, space, the
four types of categories, that is, quantity, quality, relation, modality—all of them terms which either common usage or the technical language of the traditional
logic had long since made known. Kant used these
and certain other terms to define a supposedly exhaustive list of the forms which, according to him, our intelligence imposes a priori upon all phenomena. But the
very fact that Kant especially emphasized the exhaustive character of this list, readily aroused the question:
What kind of knowledge can we possess which enables
us to be sure that just these and no others are the a priori
forms? The natural answer to this question would be:
We know these forms because they are characteristic
of the human self. Since this is our own self, we can
be sure of its forms by simply reflecting upon its nature. But this answer at once arouses a retort. The
self, as we have just seen, is, in some respects, a very
mysterious being. Yet Kant knows it well enough to be
sure what are the necessary a priori forms of its intelligence. If one turns back to his deduction of the categories to see just what, if you admit the cogency of

his main argument, he may be said to have proved in that discussion, then at best his argument seems to be that the objects of our experience must conform to whatever types of structure are in fact essential to the working of our human intelligence. This result may be fully admitted, and yet the possibility remains that in our imperfect reflections, we might be led to view as essential to the possibility of intelligent experience certain forms of conceptual structure which really are *not* essential, but which happen to be due merely to our present habits of mind. Thus, one who speaks English, and who thinks in English, has his ways of conceiving the structure of things considerably modified by the habits of English speech. In fact, Aristotle's table of categories was much influenced by considerations that were largely of a grammatical rather than of as deep a metaphysical significance as he himself supposed. In any case, such considerations as those which are mainly suggested by English or by Greek linguistic usage are not essential to the structure of the intelligence. Phenomena need not, as it were, speak to us in English nor yet in Greek forms, in order to be understood. A genuinely stable, a truly fundamental, system of categories, must therefore be founded upon considerations that are independent of language, or of any other changeable accidents of the development of human intelligence. Now one may well ask whether Kant has secured, by any articulate procedure, that his table of categories shall contain the forms really necessary to our understanding of facts, and no other—forms not accidental, merely linguistic, or otherwise conventional. If, in order to test this issue, we ask whence Kant derived his list of the necessary forms of the intelligence, the answer is that he derived his view of the forms of our sensibility, i.e., time and space, from a study of the logic of geometry as he understood that logic, while he obtained his table of the categories of the understanding in a somewhat more superficial way, viz., from a consideration of the traditional classification of judgments that the textbooks of formal logic contained. In any case, his list of the forms essential to our intelligence looks rather empirical. He gives us no reason why just these forms and no others *must* result from the very nature of a self such as ours. No one principle seems to define the whole list. His forms appear in his account without any statement of their genesis and with no acceptable discussion of the reasons for holding his list to be exhaustive. And his statement that since these are our own forms we must be able to know what they are, seems inconsistent with his equally express admission that the true nature of the self is unknown to us.

It seems impossible, then, to accept the main principles of Kant's deduction of the categories without at once proceeding to supplement that deduction. One cannot hope to know so much about the nature of the human intelligence as Kant wants us to know, without also undertaking to know more than he furnishes. If one accepts in principle the Kantian deduction, one must surely attempt to comprehend the relation of the categories to the self; and one must seek to discover a genuine unity of principle which may connect the various categories with one another, and with the time and space forms. This unity of principle, if discoverable at all, must result from something which shall prove to be knowable about the self and about its relation to experience. In substance, Kant's deduction says that the world of phenomena must conform to the type of our intelligence, because, to use a modern phrase previously employed, a certain survival of the fittest phenomena in the mental process that prepares phenomena to be known, must antedate, as it were, our own actual consciousness of any observable phenomenal facts. We can only know such phenomena as are fit to be known—an expression which contains, in fact, Kant's whole deduction in a nutshell. Such fitness presupposes an adaptation of all phenomenal facts to the essential conditions that make them intelligible, an adaption to the outline scheme which any such intelligent being as we are imposes a priori upon facts. Were facts possible that were not thus adapted to the forms of our intelligence, then we should never notice such facts as objective phenomena at all. They would perish from our experience before they were identified, or at best would remain for us mere dreams. Now if you accept this Kantian conception of the structure of experience as, in general, correct, you all the more feel the need to define just what these essential conditions of intelligibility are, and you need also to be sure of the adequacy of your definition. But since the essential is that which some principle, some reason, distinguishes from the merely accidental, you thus demand a supplementary deduction of the categories which shall show not merely the necessity of categories in general, but why *just these* categories are required by that very principle, whatever it is, upon which the entire intelligent life of the self logically depends. Some one such principle there must be, from Kant's own point of view, in case there is to be one self at all (instead of a mere variety of types of selfhood) characteristic of our human nature.

KANT'S CONCEPTION OF THE SELF

To deduce the categories from the nature of the self, and in doing so to reduce them all, and if possible, the whole of philosophy to a system of results derived from a single principle—this undertaking consequently became, for the post-Kantians, a characteristic ideal. The presence of this ideal determines the form of their systematic investigations. They do not want merely to deduce in general the applicability of our categories to all phenomena. They want to deduce each category in its order. They want to show why our intelligence demands, by virtue of some one principle of the self, the use of specific categories, and how each category determines in its place in the whole system, the structure of its own class or of its own aspect of facts.

This investigation, once attempted, almost inevitably leads to a much closer relation between the categories and the data of experience than Kant had admitted. For one thing, time and space, which Kant views as irreducible forms of our sensibility and as very distinct from the categories of the understanding, are in general considered, by the post-Kantians, as in principle inseparable from, and as definable in, terms of the categories. Moreover, even the very data of sense themselves, which Kant had regarded as an externally given material, could not escape from at least an effort, on the part of the later philosophy, to view them as also determined by the nature, although perhaps by the now hidden and unconscious nature of the self. There existed, therefore, in the view of these idealists, the need for a deduction, not indeed of the single data of sense themselves, but, in any case, of the reason why such apparently irreducible data have to be presented to the self. This deduction, if once attempted, would have to employ the same principle from whose unity the variety of the categories was also to be deduced. For otherwise philosophy would not attain that unity of system which these successors of Kant demanded. To be sure, it is false to imagine that any post-Kantian idealist ever undertook to deduce a priori the necessity that just this sound or this color or this pain should be present at a given moment to your senses. For plainly the single fact of sense can not in general be predicted except upon the basis of previous data of senses. But the effort to define from the very nature of the self, why its current experience must seem foreign to it, and why its intelligence has to be expressed in the form of a conflict with this apparently alien world of sense facts—this effort, I say, played no small part in the early idealism. Whatever you may think of the result, the effort was a natural one, for it was closely associated with the motives which, as we have now seen, led to the view that things in themselves, beyond the self, are mere fictions; so that we have to deal in philosophy, on the one hand with the phenomena, and on the other with the self, whose phenomena they are.

V.

In our sketch of the situation we have now passed in review three of the four ideas which, at the outset of this lecture, we regarded as summing up the sense of the Kantian deduction. The view that we know phenomena, and not things in themselves, the accompanying assertion that we know the a priori forms of the intelligence, the thesis that these forms are imposed a priori upon the matter which the senses furnish, while nevertheless the forms do not, of themselves, predetermine this matter which fills them out—these features of Kant's doctrine inevitably led, as we have seen, to new reflections, and so to modifications of his theses. The things in themselves become of so problematic a nature that they come to appear useless furniture of which philosophy must rid itself. Or if any such concept is, for the idealists, to survive at all, it must survive, as would seem, in the shape of whatever is at the heart or at the root of the self. The categories require a new deduction, which shall, if possible, connect them with time, with space, with one another, and with the self, according to some single principle which shall determine how the self needs just these forms. The source of the very matter of sense itself must be brought, if possible, into some relation with the nature of the self, and with the single principle just mentioned, in such a manner that it may become evident why the self needs, after all, to view its own realm of sense facts as an alien realm, even in order to win it over, through intelligent articulation, to some conscious unity with the purpose of the reason. In other words, whatever principle is at the basis of self-consciousness must, if possible, be shown to be also the principle that lies at the basis of the sense world. Thus only could Kant's philosophy be rendered satisfactory to the very minds which took the warmest interest in its fashion of analyzing experience.

The fourth one in our list of the characteristic thoughts of Kant's deduction still remains to be considered. This was the thought that all our possible experience must be viewed as connected and as interrelated, by virtue of the very fact that it is to be defined as the experience of one virtual self. This virtual self appears to be not merely the intelligent observer, from moment to moment, of each passing fact, but also the possessor, in some sense, of all facts at once. "There is," said Kant, "but one experience," and all experiences are to be viewed as parts of this one experience. Here was a thought which Kant had emphasized, but which he had also kept, after a fashion very characteristic of his own habits of suspended judgment, in a state of deliberately arrested development.

Whatever possible experience I acknowledge—let us say, an experience of the physical state of the interior of the earth, or of a remote event in the past history of the cosmos—I acknowledge that fact only by placing it in the same virtual unity of experience in which my present observations have their place. So teaches Kant. Thereby he defines, as he believes, that sort and degree of objectivity in phenomena which the logic of empirical science demands. Knowledge is only of things experienced. But knowledge is not concerned merely with the here and now of experience. Knowledge is concerned with the relation of every phenomenon to the whole of experience.

Now who has this whole of experience? Not I, in so far as here and now I observe facts. In the whole of experience, your experience, and the experiences of Galileo, of Newton, of whoever has observed or is yet to observe phenomena, have their places. Experience is no private affair. It belongs to all human kind. We share in it as we share in a common national existence or in a common humanity. The knowing self which is viewed as the one subject of experience must at least virtually be viewed as the self of mankind, rather than as the transient intelligent activity of any mortal amongst us.

KANT'S CONCEPTION OF THE SELF

Kant repeatedly, in effect although never in quite as express words as I have just used, indicates that we can only deal with the objective facts of human science by regarding all human experience as if it constituted a single whole. It is, to my mind, equally clear that this unity remains for Kant a virtual unity, never anything in which he believes as a concrete and conscious mental reality. *How* the mental processes of various men are ultimately and metaphysically related to one another, Kant does not know. That remains among the insoluble mysteries of the hidden real nature of things. But when we believe any observed physical phenomena to be objectively real, we regard our own empirical judgments, made regarding such observed facts, as valid for all men. A judgment about experience is valid, according to Kant, because the conditions which determine the unity of a man's consciousness require it to be valid. It must follow that what we view as the conditions which determine our own unity of consciousness we also view as the conditions which determine the unity of every other man's consciousness. Moreover, all the objective empirical facts which are valid for any of us, each of us views as bound up in a single unity of experience, namely his own unity. This single unity must then be virtually the same for all men, since any man's objective empirical facts are, if rightly defined, valid for every other man. How one can thus view this virtual unity as genuine, without conceiving the intelligent selves of all men as constituting the expression of an actually and concretely real selfhood, wherein all men share, does not and cannot appear from Kant's carefully guarded expressions. This point also was one upon which he simply kept his judgment suspended. It was natural, therefore, that one of the problems of the later idealism should be the relation of the individual human self to the other intelligent human selves.

Herewith we touch upon one, although not upon the only motive that strongly influences the later idealists to use, in addition to the term self, another term, viz., the term Absolute. We have already seen how the concept of the self, as Kant had defined that term, deepened its significance as one reflected upon the manifold offices which the self had to fulfil in later philosophy. The self is the knower whose categories predetermine the form of all phenomena. The self is also the doer whose acts have a more than phenomenal meaning. The self has, in addition, a nature that, although single and united, determines a variety of categories in accordance with some unity of principle which philosophy must attempt to define. Yet further, the self has a fundamental nature which must, at least in general, determine not only the form but in some still hidden sense the very matter of experience. But now, above all, this concept of the self must be so enriched as to become not merely individual but social. For we all, not merely any one individual alone, are its offspring and its expression.

To such postulates the post-Kantian idealists were led by a process whose logic I have thus endeavored to sketch. You may think what you will of their results. It is interesting to remark, even at this stage of our inquiry, that their most significant subsequent work was related to the matter to which we have just alluded. The post-Kantian idealism was noteworthy in its analysis of the conditions of knowledge. But as we shall find in the sequel, it was still more noteworthy in its development of social concepts, and in its decidedly fruitful study of the relations which bind the individual self to that unity of selfhood which includes all individuals.

The idealists have been much ridiculed by their critics for their use of the term "The Absolute." It may interest us to learn that one of the chief motives for substituting the term "Absolute" for the term "self" as the name for the principle of philosophy, was interwoven with motives furnished by the social consciousness. For whatever else the later idealism proved to be, we shall find that it included, as one of its most notable parts, a social philosophy. And whoever wishes to understand modern social doctrines, will do well to take account of the contribution to that sort of thinking which was made by idealism.

Note to Lecture II.

[The editor finds the author's following criticism of Kant here pertinent. The passage is from an early unpublished fragment entitled "Some Characteristics of Being."]

Kant has an ontology. The recognition of the things in themselves as obvious presuppositions is, for him, an essential part of the doctrine which sets definite limits to our knowledge, and which declares the things in themselves unknowable. Nor does the Kantian ontology cease with the mere recognition of the things in themselves. In various ways these unknowable realities become, as it were, inevitably entangled in the fortunes of the world of knowledge. And one of the most curious instances of this entanglement appears in the Kantian theory of the process whereby knowledge itself comes to be constituted.

The definitive form of the critical theory of knowledge, as appears from the well-known letter to Herz, had its origin in a reflection upon a certain specific ontological situation to which Kant's attention had been attracted immediately after the discovery of the antinomies, and the consequent abandonment of any reality for time and space beyond the knowing mind's sensuous constitution had led Kant to feel himself as it were more estranged from the realm of the noumena. In consequence of this sense of estrangement, Kant was led to say: If the realities beyond and the understanding within are thus essentially, and of course ontologically sundered, as in separate realms of being, how is the relation of knowledge to its object possible at all? For Kant at this stage, then, as for so many other thinkers, the epistemological problem is subordinate to the ontological theory. Knower and noumenon are, as beings, apart from one another. And it is supposed to be known that this situation is a fact. The epistemology does not first prove to the thinker this ontological result; rather is the epistemology invented to meet issues suggested by the ontological presupposition. "Allein," says Kant, "unser Verstand ist durch seine Vorstellungen weder die Ursache des Gegenstandes (ausser in der Moral von den guten Zwecken), noch der Gegenstand die Ursache der Verstandesvorstellungen (in sensu reali). Die reinen Verstandesbegriffe müssen . . . in der Natur der Seele zwar ihre Quellen haben, aber doch weder insofern sie vom Object gewirkt werden, noch das Object selbst hervorbringen. Ich hatte mich in der Dissertation damit begnügt die Natur der Intellectual-Vorstellungen bloss negativ auszudrücken: dass sie nämlich nicht Modificationen der Seele durch den Gegenstand wären. Wie aber denn sonst eine Vorstellung, die sich auf einen Gegenstand bezieht, ohne von ihm auf einige Weise afficirt zu sein, möglich, überging ich mit Stillschweigen." To the question thus raised, Kant devoted himself thenceforth during the elaboration of his new critical doctrine.

But if the presupposition of the new epistemology was ontological, the further procedure was not less so. Everyone knows that complex and in some respects variable doctrine of the way in which *Verstand, Sinnlichkeit, Einbildungskraft,* and finally *Vernunft,* coöperate to bring to pass the structure which the critical doctrine calls human knowledge, the various grades of "synthesis," the "hidden" operations of the *Einbildungskraft,* the list of categories, the perplexing doctrine of the Schema. Now the result of all this theory is well known—the situation in which it leaves human experience, the limitation and the correlated necessities of the empirical sciences, the new type of objectivity which Kant defines, in his theory of *Mögliche Erfahrung*—in brief, the whole teaching concerning our cognitive relations to reality which Kant so significantly sets forth as his critical outcome. But many a reader has noted, with a perplexity not easily to be satisfied through any study of Kant's text, one question which the entire discussion raises, but always keeps in the background. Such, Kant tells us, is the limitation of knowledge, because such is the process by means of which knowledge comes to pass. Sense affects, apprehension beholds, sense-forms embrace, imagination, toiling as it were in the dark, schematizes, categories consequently pervade the whole material of experience. There results an ordered whole, full of a transcendental affinity of fact and fact, a whole centered about the ever possible thought "It is I who think thus." This whole, always more or less ideal, a life-plan, as it were, but never a completed career for our understanding, is the realm of experience, a fruitful and well-ordered island in the ocean of ontological mysteries. This then is our kingdom of knowledge. This it is, because thus it is made. Yes, one asks, but this process that makes knowledge, is it a real process, or only a seeming process? Has the process any being of its own, or is it only an ideal construction of the philosopher? The answer must be in one sense obvious enough. The process occurs. It is real. Because it has being, and true being, the realm of knowledge has such constitution as belongs to it, and such limits as Kant defines. But once again: Is this type of being which the process possesses the noumenal type, or only a phenomenal type? Is it only a matter of *Mögliche Erfahrung* that such a process is found to take place? Or does the noumenal ego in any sense participate in the process? To this question a satisfactory answer seems hard, upon a Kantian basis, to find.

If one goes back to the original ontological presuppositions of the critical theory, one finds the answer to our question involving considerations that appear to belong largely, if not wholly, to the realm of ultimate or noumenal being. Originally, the problem of the letter to Herz ran, as we have seen, thus: It is presupposed that there are two beings, or rather two realms of being, the *Gegenstände* proper, and the knowing subject. Now the latter, the knowing subject, pretends to be aware of certain *Verstandesbegriffe* which tell him about the *Gegenstände wie sie an sich sind*. But the *Gegenstände* do not affect the understanding of the knowing subject, and so do not directly mould the latter to their own form. How then is the knowledge possible? The critical answer runs that, as a fact, no true knowledge of the *Gegenstände an sich* is possible, since they, unquestionably real as they remain, cannot get into the knowing subject's realm of experience. As a fact, the knowing subject's realm of knowledge is the result of his own nature, which, by virtue of its mechanism aforesaid, builds up the structure of experience, coherent, and relatively objective, but still inner.

That the knowing subject, however, has this mechanism, that his powers do thus build up his experience by the application of a priori forms, this would seem to be itself an ontological assertion upon the same level as the original ontological assertions with which we started. We have learned to know that we do not know the *Gegenstände an sich,* because we have also learned to know better than we did one real process whose being is as genuine as is that of the original noumena themselves. This is the process whereby our own experience gets its structure. This process occurs. The constitution of the island, and the waves that limit its shores, these are as real as are the hidden wonders of the unknown ocean beyond. And unless the process whereby the nature and limits of knowledge get their constitution thus possesses as genuine a being as do the noumena themselves, it would apparently be hard to make out in what sense the Kantian doctrine of the limitations of knowledge can be called a really true doctrine at all.

This seems to be one answer to our question. But the fact seems to be equally clear that many aspects of Kant's own theory forbid the acceptance of this answer as sufficient from his own point of view. The whole spirit of the Kantian deduction of the categories, especially in its later forms, tends to set over against this purely ontological interpretation of the basis of his epistemology, a far more decidedly immanent theory according to which the true limitation of knowledge is discovered by a process of internal reflection. This immanent theory, in so far as Kant indicates its scope, assumes several fairly distinct forms. According to one form, we discover the limitations of knowledge by reflecting that science everywhere uses certain a priori principles, whose necessity conditions the very possibility of science, while no mere collection of experience could warrant, and no preëstablished harmony of knowledge and of noumenal being could adequately establish them. But science is, within the realm of human experience, an immanent, but still even as such, an unquestionable fact. Hence science must be possible. As, from the nature of necessary truth, known to us a priori, no commerce with things in themselves could make science possible, the necessity of the principles of science must be itself immanent, while of things in themselves there can be no science.

While this fashion of interpreting the basis of Kant's theory does not wholly avoid (as what discussion can avoid?) existential predicates, it does indeed, as far as it goes, tend to free the Kantian epistemology from logical dependence upon the original ontology, and tends to make Kant's hypotheses as to the processes whereby knowledge gets organized, hypotheses whose warrant is to be obtained, if at all, either within the field of psychological experience upon the one hand, or by the aid of general epistemological reflection upon the other. The only trouble with this aspect of the doctrine is the arbitrariness of the epistemological presupposition that science, with necessary a priori principles, must be possible —an assumption which Kant never sufficiently maintains against a possible skepticism.

Kant makes, however, yet other efforts to set his epistemology upon an independent basis. The efforts grouped about the central idea of the Transcendental Unity of Apperception are the deepest. But into these we cannot here go. Suffice it to say that upon this side Kant goes far to break the ontological chains in which he had first bound himself. Yet his theory, as he expounds it, never fully attains the freedom at which Kant unconsciously aimed. To the end it remains true that, as Kant states his case, his theory of knowledge generally is made to appear dependent upon an assertion that the processes whereby knowledge is formed are real facts in the realm of being, a being that might as well be called as genuine as are the very noumena from whose presence Kant intends to banish us altogether.

In so far, however, as this is the case, Kant also is condemned to his own decidedly disheartening form of our process of circular proof and of circular definition, so far as relates to his ontology. For if his theory of knowledge is dependent upon his assumption of the existence of a certain ontological situation, it is true that Kant's theory, once accepted, forbids us to define any ontological situation whatever except as purely problematic accounts of what can have for us no *Bedeutung*, no true meaning whatever. In Kant's case then the circle is that, in order to reach his epistemology, as he usually states the latter, one has to accept his ontology, while after one has once accepted the epistemology, anything but a wholly problematic ontology is excluded. Or again, in Kant's case, one defines true or noumenal being as that which cannot be known because such and such is the structure of knowledge, while one argues that this account of the structure of knowledge is true, partly at least because one has first assumed that such and such a real process, a process as real as the noumenal being itself from which one started, is taking place, and is limiting knowledge to this or to that field.

LECTURE III.

THE CONCEPT OF THE ABSOLUTE AND
THE DIALECTICAL METHOD.

MY former lecture was devoted to a general study of the transition from Kant's view of the self to that deeper but more problematic conception of the self which characterized the later idealism. Before characterizing further that conception, let me first remind you of some of the external conditions under which the German philosophical thinking of the time now in question took place.

I.

Kant published his *Critique of Pure Reason* in 1771. The next ten years were marked by the first reception of that book in Germany, by the earliest efforts to understand, to expound, to criticize, and to supplement Kant's doctrines, and also by the appearance of the most important of Kant's own further expositions of his principal philosophical teaching. In 1792 the literary career of Fichte began; and in 1794 that philosopher published the first statement of his own form of idealism, in his *Wissenschaftslehre*. Almost at the same moment the young Schelling set out upon his career of rapid, brilliant, and changeful expressions of doctrine. In the last year of the century, Hegel's professional career as a teacher of philosophy began, when he went as *Privat-*

Docent to Jena; and his own characteristic teachings received their first extended formulation in his *Phae-nomenologie des Geistes,* published in 1807. All these works were, at the moment, but single examples of a very large philosophical literature which Germany was producing in those years.

We are here concerned with the beginnings of idealism. It requires only a moment's reflection upon the great historical events that were contemporary with this remarkable outburst of philosophical activity, to remind us what manner of time that was. In a general sketch of the philosophical situation of those years, I have indicated, in my *Spirit of Modern Philosophy,* some of the relations of the philosophical to the literary movement of that period in Germany, and I have also endeavored in that book to characterize some of the personalities who were concerned in both movements. It is not my purpose to repeat here in any detail these more popular aspects of the early history of idealism. But I do not wish you to lose sight of the fact that the abstract thinking whose fortunes we are trying to portray, was inevitably, and quite normally, a reflection of the tendencies and of the problems of the civilization of just that age. I beg you to keep this fact in mind as you follow these lectures, whenever the problems and the theories of the philosophers seem to you, for the moment, hopelessly remote and unreal. Philosophy and life were then in far closer touch than, as I fear, they are today in the minds of many people. All this technical speech of categories and of knowledge, of phenomena and of the self, of the individual and of the Absolute—all this speech, I say, was rendered vital to the philosophically disposed readers of that time by the fact that, to their minds, it bore upon the very life problems which the Revolution and the new social ideals and the passions of the romantic movement made so prominent.

Kant's first Critique had won so wide a public hearing in Germany, in the eighties of the eighteenth century, largely because of the emphasis which its happily chosen title put upon the interests of the human reason. The word *reason* was to the age that immediately antedated the French Revolution very much what the word evolution has been to our own generation—a sort of general comforter of all those who felt puzzled and longed for light. Whatever the issue, the enlightened souls of that time said, "Reason will set us right." Reason was to be the all-powerful substitute for religion, tradition, superstition, authority, custom, prejudice, oppression, in brief for whatever man happened to view as a galling harness. Reason was to be a chain breaker, jail deliverer, world reformer. Thus, when Kant undertook in his Critique an exhaustive survey of the province, the powers, and the limits of the reason, he had in his favor not merely technical but also deep-seated popular interests. So he won a well-deserved attention.

The results of Kant's Critique seemed to many disappointingly negative. But then, that was an age of great destructions. When the Revolution came, many institutions which had long seemed to be things in themselves, showed that they were nothing but phenomena. And when new constitutions and new social orders had to be planned, the spirit of the age emphasized the fact that, at least in the social world, it is the office of the human intelligence to impose its own forms upon the phenomena, and to accept no authority but that of the rational self. So in that day the spirit of the Kantian philosophy reflected, in a very practical sense, the tendencies of the age. The destructive as well as the constructive features of this new philosophy were in harmony with that reforming spirit in consequence of which the word *reason* at length became, as the Revolutionary ideals matured, not a mere name, but a term for a great regulative force, whose value lay no longer in its vaguely abstract authority but in its creative power, in its capacity to mould plastic phenomena into conformity with its forms.

The transition from Kant's philosophy to the later idealism was again a reflection of the spirit which determined the course of contemporary social events. Three features marked the mental life in Germany during the decades with which the eighteenth century closed and the nineteenth century opened, say from 1770 to 1805. The first feature was the great development of actual productive power in scholarship, in literature, in imaginative work generally, and the accompanying increase in the popular respect for great individuals. This tendency is visible from 1770 until the close of the old century. The second feature was that deepening of sentiment, that enrichment of emotional life, which characterized first the storm and stress period, and later both the classical and the romantic literatures of Germany in those decades. The third feature was that relative indifference to mere political fortunes, that spirit of world-citizenship, that fondness for what Jean Paul called ''the empire of the air,'' which by the close of the old century became so characteristic of the most representative Germans at the very time when, as the Napoleonic period began, the national unity and even the political existence of Germany seemed to be hopelessly lost. These three features of German mental life had a close connection with the great social movements of that period. The spirit of the revolutionary age, even before 1789, had set free the great individuals. The intense social activities of Europe after the political revolution began, found their expression, in Germany, not indeed for the time in effective political reconstructions, but rather in the form of a vast increase both of scholarly and of imaginatively creative mental life. Meanwhile this age of great experiences not unnaturally became also an age of great romantic emotions, in which Germany, by virtue of the temperament of her people, led the way. And at a period when political and military successes proved to be impossible for the divided Germany as it then was, the representative leaders of German public opinion preserved their spiritual independence, protected their individuality by deliberately ignoring, or else by defying political fortunes, in brief by aiming to show their moral superiority to the external mishaps of their country. This was the age and the land for a somewhat unpractical and fantastical idealism. It was also the land and the age for really great thoughts, whose influence in later times and in other forms will be permanent.

Two topics were thus rendered especially prominent in the minds of representative German thinkers, whether they were technical philosophers or not. The first was the self, not merely what we now call the empirical ego of psychology, but the significant self, the hero of the storm and stress literature of the seventies and eighties, and of the romantic emotions of later literary art, the sovereign of the new spiritual order—the self that could rise above fortune and win without external aid. The second was what one may call, in a well-known sense, the invisible world in which the self is immersed—the realm into which Goethe's Faust seeks to penetrate at the outset of the poem—the region, namely, of ideal truths, of truths which you do not so much discover through observing either physical or political facts, as by investigating moral and æsthetic truth, and by consulting what you may at first imagine to be magic powers.

So far as the self was prominent in the minds of the Germans of that time, the tendencies of the age were towards a somewhat romantic type of individualism. Goethe's *Faust* in its earliest form, Schiller's early dramas, Goethe's *Prometheus,* Friederich Schlegel's romantic irony, Fichte's popular work called the *Vocation of Man*—these are representative expressions of the various sorts of individualism to which this period sooner or later gave birth. Such individualism was seldom of the type which Nietzsche has in our own days emphasized. The well-known doctrine of Nietzsche is that of an individual equally merciless to himself and to others. It is a restlessly intolerant and muscular individualism which despises its own sufferings, an idealism without any ideal world of truth, a religion without a faith, a martyrdom without prospect of a paradise. But this individualism of the storm and stress, of the classical and of the romantic periods of German literature was always, in the first instance, an emotional rather than what one might call a motor individualism; and it had great faith in its own discoveries of ideal truths. Its excesses were much more sentimental than are those of Nietzsche, and it usually had a religious faith, unorthodox but glowing. It might be rebellious; it might even undertake, in ideal forms, world-destroying revolutionary enterprises. But it never really despised its own affairs of the heart, as

Nietzsche proudly despises his own emotional illusions. On the contrary, the individualism of that time always sought great heart experiences, and generally believed in them, whereas, in our day, individualism loves to assume a more drastic and contemptuous tone, where the interests of the heart are concerned. When German individualism, in those romantic old days, was philosophical and reflective, it might be highly critical; but it was withal, in the end, either fantastically or even laboriously constructive, rather than mainly iconoclastic, whereas our extreme individualists are fond of making, as it were, pyramids of the skulls of their enemies. Individualism is indeed always strongly negative, but the individualism of that time had its hearty positive enthusiasms, and often hugged its very illusions. It destroyed, but it was fond also of building its own temples, which were often indeed rather too much in the air.

As for the other topic of that time, the ideal world, that of course has often attracted the eager interest of the cultivated minds of mankind. The ideal world for the German thinkers of those days differed from that of Plato, as well as from that of mediæval tradition. This new realm of the ideal was first of all a region where great ethical interests were prominent, but these interests had modern forms, determined by the social struggles of the age. Freedom, the ideal social order of modern society, the ideals of beauty suggested by the newer romantic poetry—these were among the notable problems of this time. So far as one went beyond the individual, the mysterious linkage of the self to other selves and to the whole universe of being, formed the central problem of philosophy. The religious views of the time meanwhile became altered; and instead of the God of traditional theology, and also instead of the world-contriving and utilitarian divine being of the earlier eighteenth century deism, one now sought for the Abso-lute—a being characterized in that time by two princi-pal attributes: first, that the Absolute was impersonal and thus relatively pantheistic in type; while, secondly, the self was nevertheless the best image and revelation, the true incarnation, of this Absolute. This paradox, that the self was the center of the universe, while the Absolute was nevertheless impersonal, formed the crucial issue of the time.

II.

I am thus led from this general sketch of the state of German mental life in the years in question, back to the properly philosophical field.

The early idealists, then, made the problems of philosophy center about two principal conceptions, that of the self and that of the Absolute. We have seen how these thinkers, in so far as they were guided by their technical interests, came by the first of these problems. The Kantian deduction of the categories had given this problem of the self its new form, and had done so by emphasizing the fact that all phenomena (and phenomena, alone, according to Kant, are knowable) are inevitably moulded in their form by the conditions which are imposed upon them by the self in order that they may become known to this self. As soon, however, as thinkers had undertaken to look closer into Kant's problem, to see why the self has these categories, and no others, and to understand how the self imposes these categories upon the data of sense, it had become obvious that Kant's account of the matter was incomplete. The self remained even for Kant a problem. Kant's own emphasis, in his later writings, upon the ethical aspects of the self, still further made it necessary to understand where the basis and the true unity of self-consciousness lies. And when the philosophers further attacked this problem of the self, their interest was intensified by the whole spirit of an age which, as we have now seen, believed in the self, believed in individuality, gloried in the inner life.

We have now also seen why the other problem—the problem of the Absolute—was almost equally emphasized by the interests of that day. Whatever the true self is, its nature is hidden, at least from our ordinary knowledge, in the depths of unconsciousness. Only when we learn to reflect can we hope to penetrate any of its deeper mysteries. But when we reflect, we at once bring to light a new question, the question of the relations between the practical and the theoretical life of the self. The two expressions of self-consciousness, ''I know,'' and ''I do,'' stand, in Kant's account, in a profoundly baffling relation. The unity can here be found only through some principle which Kant left still undiscovered. Closely connected with this problem is another which Kant indeed touches but only to leave it for his successors to develop. This problem is furnished by the relations amongst the many selves. That they possess a common nature, is implied in every step of Kant's discussion of the human intellect. How this common nature is to be further defined, this matter Kant treats with a careful reticence. What indications he gives are paradoxically baffling. Kant's ideal moral world of rational agents—the object of what he defines as our well-warranted faith—is a realm of ethical autonomy, a kingdom of free selves, a distinctly pluralistic community, as Professor Howison has, with historical accuracy, insisted. The virtual self of the deduction of the categories, however, is a principle whose unity determines the mutual relations of all possible human experiences, and whose universality defines the sense in which empirical judgments are valid for all men. If you give to this principle any further definition than Kant had given it, the unity of this true ego invites a monistic formulation. Kant has no reason to decide between such a monism and his ethical pluralism. The one is a concept of his theory of knowledge, the other of his ethics. And ultimate truth we cannot know. His judgment in these matters is theoretically suspended. But for his idealistic successors such deliberate suspension of judgment proved impossible. We thus begin to see why, in view of the conflict between the unity of the world of truth and the pluralism of the world of action, these idealists were led to seek a solution in terms of the conception of an impersonal Absolute, which is nevertheless the ground and the source of personality.

It would of course be inaccurate to ascribe to the concept of the Absolute as these men formed it the sole office of accounting for the relations of various selves. Unquestionably the magnitude of the social movements of those times, the vast changes of civilization that were then under way, the elemental passions that were then set free, the sense of an overwhelming fate, predetermining human affairs—all these things influenced the philosophers in their conception of the Absolute. In sharp contrast to the individualism of the revolutionary period, stood the fact of the blind power of the mob, which the Revolution had for a while so impressively demonstrated. The general awakening of the peoples, viewed as great masses, was as notable a fact of the age as was the importance of the heroes of the day. Napoleon, when he came, seemed to his admirers less a mere individual than the incarnation of some demonic spirit of a whole nation's life. The hackneyed story relates how Hegel, who one day saw Napoleon for a moment after the battle of Jena, said that he had met the *Weltgeist zu Pferde.* In those days, one could not long remain merely individualistic. The self was prominent; but the universe was impressing upon the beholder, in a new way, its possession of vast impersonal forces which used individuals as their mere tools. In the light of such experiences men began to read the philosophy of history in a new way.

Nevertheless, something more than the social and historical problems impelled thinkers towards an interpretation of the world in terms of an Absolute. Kant's theory was, within its carefully guarded limits, a doctrine regarding the bases of our empirical knowledge of phenomena. It was no theory of nature. Our understanding determines forms; it cannot predetermine the material that shall fill these forms. Hence nature remains to us a mystery. We can never deduce a single concrete fact. Why, for instance, organisms exist in nature with the appearance of having been designed, we can never hope to fathom through our understanding. Kant once more resolutely suspends his judgments. We can understand the order of phenomena; we can never pierce to the heart of things and find why they exist.

The idealists could not accept this Kantian limitation. Once they had disposed of Kant's shadowy and unknowable things in themselves, the problem of the world became for them, as we have seen, one about the true nature of the self. This problem, however, sent them far beneath the threshold of our ordinary consciousness.

Whatever it is that determines the experience of the self, must also determine not only all of the forms and the relations of the many selves but also the true basis of all the phenomena that appear to us as physical nature. Grant that the physical world is a phenomenon, *our* phenomenon. Then it is our own deeper nature which determines this phenomenon to appear thus foreign to us, and ourselves to seem as if we were mere products of its mechanism. All experience is appearance for the self. Well then, we must be able, if we reflect rightly, to discover, not indeed the reason for every detail of the world, but at least the general reasons why our experience presents to us here the organic and there the inorganic type of phenomena, here the growth of things, and there their decay. We must be able to learn why it is, and in what sense, that the individual man appears and must appear to us as a phenomenon amongst phenomena, as a product of nature—in brief, why man, who bears about in his own inmost core the very secret of the universe of phenomena, still seems, and has to seem, as if he were the mere creature of a day, whom a mere wound can destroy, whom a pestilence can slay. In sum then, this philosophy must undertake to be a philosophy of nature, and to discuss, not merely the forms of things, but their presentation, source, and meaning.

I suggest thus in outline certain of the main thoughts of this philosophical movement, attempting at this point neither criticism nor defense of these thoughts. They were at least a natural product of the situation. And one sees why a philosophy which was equally to explain our own inner as well as the basis of our experience of outer nature, was readily disposed to attempt to unify its notions by means of an impersonal conception of the

THE CONCEPT OF THE ABSOLUTE

Absolute, a conception still to be kept in the closest touch with the conception of the true meaning of the self.

In addition to the problems of the self, of the many selves, and of nature, the philosophy of this time was deeply moved by the new form which the problems of religion had inevitably received in consequence of the spirit of the age. Individualism had broken with theological authority. The eighteenth century worship of reason had long since rendered rationalism in theology a favorite philosophical ideal. The Kantian philosophy, in relegating religion to the position of an indemonstrable ideal, to be purified into a simply rational faith in God, freedom, and immortality, had only the more set free the tendency to reconstruct the contents of tradition in accordance with the spirit of the time. The new conception of the Absolute was thus inevitably developed under the influence of a predisposition in favor of a new theology. There is a profoundly religious motive which, both in Hindoo and in Western thought, has for thousands of years underlain the view that one comes into closest touch with the Divine, not without but within one's own true self. The Hindoo seers and the Christian mystics had agreed in seeking an unity of the self and of the Divine wherein the nature of each is intimately revealed at the moment when they are nearest together. The new idealism revived these ancient thoughts but gave them its own form. What is at the heart, at the root, at the ground of the self, must be, in terms of the philosophy of which Kant's doctrine had given such novel forms, the Absolute, the common root and ground of all selfhood, and of all nature. This then, so these thinkers hold, will be what the ancient faith has meant by the name ''God.'' Only the new philosophy will be no merely mystical experience. It will be a well-wrought and systematic doctrine, with a method of its own. A revised and completed deduction of the categories shall render the new formulation of religious faith compatible with reason. The triumph of the new age shall thus be the union of the "form" of a new rationalism with the "matter" of ancient mysticism. Such, I say, is in general the ideal of the religious philosophy to which this time gave birth.

III.

You have now before you a few of the fundamental ideas of the philosophy of this period. We must next suggest something regarding the method of thinking which became characteristic of this philosophy. Concerning this method a great deal of misunderstanding exists amongst those who are not acquainted with the matter at first hand. These Germans, one says, attempted to evolve all things out of their inner consciousness. So much, and no more, does one, only too frequently, know about what went on in the procedure of the early idealistic metaphysicians. Those who thus sum up the whole matter are accustomed to conceive our idealists merely as imaginative persons who fancied whatever they pleased, and who then hid from themselves and their pupils the arbitrariness of their opinions by means of much unintelligible phraseology. The one amongst the greater early idealists who gave most ground for such an opinion was Schelling, a genius, but in his youth an unprincipled and voluble genius, who began to write with enormous rapidity when he was twenty, and who had reached the culmination of his most productive period, and of his influence, before he had well passed thirty years of age. No doubt Schelling at his worst is indeed an arbitrarily imaginative person; his early won fame intoxicated him, he lacked due self-criticism, and he did not take the trouble properly to digest his large store of information concerning the current physical science of his day, while he nevertheless attempted to use this information for the purpose of constructing a new Philosophy of Nature. The result is that he wrote much upon this topic which remains both fruitless and unreadable. Yet even in the course of such hasty work, Schelling often showed a fine instinct for essentially important leading ideas such as the science of his day was beginning to develop. Some few of his own leading ideas in regard to nature are of decidedly more importance than the first glance indicates.*

However, it is no part of my task at this moment to discriminate at all exhaustively between the good and the bad in the methods of thinking used here or there by Schelling or by any other of the thinkers of the time. What is here needed is a broad outline of the most novel, most characteristic, and least arbitrary of the methods which these philosophers gradually developed. This was the so-called dialectical or antithetical method. It meant much more than any purely arbitrary use of the constructive imagination. It did not consist of anything that can be fairly described as an evolving of the facts out of one's inner consciousness, in so far as that phrase suggests mere fancifulness. This method, on the contrary, had a certain very marked exactness of its own. Used within due limits it will always remain a valuable in-

* Cf. the author's "Relations between Philosophy and Science in the First Half of the Nineteenth Century." *Science*, N. S., XXXVIII, 1913, pp. 567-584.—ED.

strument of philosophical thought. Let me try to indicate at this point the nature of this dialectical method.

Historically speaking, this method is derived from Socrates, and elaborated in the Platonic dialogues, especially in the *Parmenides,* and to some extent in the *Sophist,* in the *Phædo,* in the *Theætetus,* in the *Phædrus* and elsewhere. As Plato used it, it often consists in developing and then comparing antithetical, i.e., mutually contradictory, doctrines, partly for the sake of leading the way, through natural, or perhaps inevitable, preliminary errors, to some truth which lies beyond them, and partly for the sake of exhibiting a complex truth in its various aspects, by looking at it first from one side and then from another in order finally to win a combined view of the whole. Thus, in the *Theætetus,* the Socrates of the dialogue aims towards the goal of a sound definition of knowledge—a goal which is indeed not reached in the dialogue—by first setting aside, through an elaborate dialectical process, the natural preliminary error of defining knowledge as sense impression. In the introduction to the *Republic,* false views of the nature of justice are expounded in order to clear the way for the true definition. On the other hand, in the *Phædrus* two views of nature and the effects of love are set in antithesis in order even thereby to depict the truth which justifies both views. This truth is that there is a conflict in the human soul of the two natures, the lower and the higher, and that hereby our mortal lives and our future destinies are determined. Love is a soul-destroying madness. Love is also a godlike passion, a divine madness, whereby we learn our true destiny. The conflict between these two theses is depicted, in this dialogue, as simply the abstract expression of the moral conflict of life, the warfare of the spirit with the flesh.

In addition to such more formal opposition of thesis and antithesis, the dialectical process plays, in Socratic dialogues, the general part of moving principle of the whole discussion. Through a constant self-analysis of its own defects, our thinking is led to what often appears in the dialogues to be its only possible mode of self-expression. Without erring, and transcending our error, we, as sometimes suggested by the Socratic irony, simply cannot become wise. Such is human wisdom; namely the self-consciousness that observes one's own forms of unwisdom. Without such self-consciousness, one remains blind in one's own conceit. Yet to get it, one must err and then rise above the error.

The thought thus somewhat dimly indicated by various Socratic expressions in the Platonic dialogues—the thought that error is not a mere accident of an untrained intellect, but a necessary stage or feature or moment of the expression of the truth as it is in itself—this thought is the very one which the idealists of our period not merely admit, but consciously emphasize, and develop in new forms. Without the Platonic dialogues this dialectical method would indeed never have existed. But one cannot say that our idealists merely took over the old method and applied it to new problems. On the contrary, in the end they so revised it as to lead them to the thesis that philosophical truth is, as they gradually came to say, essentially dialectical, i.e., you cannot express the highest insights except in the form of a series of antitheses. Although, as I have suggested, the Platonic dialogues contain indications of such a tendency, Plato's own conception of ultimate truth tends to make the dialectical process appear rather an incident of our human life than a necessity of the truth as it exists in the pure realm of the Ideas themselves. Such evidences as Plato emphasizes for the thesis that the Ideas themselves are the result of a dialectical process, remain undeveloped. These idealists, however, devote a great deal of space to making the dialectical aspect of truth very explicit.

The new form of the dialectical method was also due, in part, to Kant's famous doctrine of the antinomies. Kant undertook to show that the human reason becomes involved in conflicts whenever it attempts to discuss the beginning of the world in time, the limits of the world in space, the ultimate divisibility or non-divisibility of matter, the possibility of the free initiation of a series of causes and effects, or the existence of a necessary being. Thus one can demonstrate, with equal cogency, that if the real world is in time at all, it must have had a beginning, yet cannot have had a beginning. If the real world is in space, it must be limited, and with equal cogency can be proved to be unlimited; and so on. Kant states these antinomies and the argument for both theses and antitheses and then shows that the solution depends upon distinguishing between the world of things in themselves and the world of phenomena. Kant's solution need not here further concern us. We know that it could not content our idealists, who did not admit the validity of the Kantian distinction here in question. But the fact that Kant declared the appearance of these antitheses to be essential to the very life of the human reason, so that the reason, according to him, always expresses itself in these antithetical demands upon our conceptual powers, was of more importance for the idealists. For them the question consequently tends to take this form: Whatever the solution of any antinomy, why do such antinomies, real or apparent, arise in our minds at all? Why do we not come at the truth directly, or else, if ignorance besets us, why do we not become directly, or through our mere failures to get light, conscious of our ignorance? Why are there regions of our thinking where conflicting judgments appear to us to possess an equally cogent evidence, so that it is to us as if both a thesis and an antithesis were positively true?

No one could be interested in such a question unless he had cases of apparently dialectical or antithetical thinking prominently before his mind, and unless such instances seemed to him no results of merely accidental or easily avoidable blunders. The idealists actually believed themselves to be in possession of such notable cases. Moreover they came to regard such cases as characteristic of philosophical thought, and, in fact, of philosophical truth. Still holding ourselves free from any prejudgment of the merits of this view of philosophical truth, let us now endeavor merely to illustrate some of the forms of the dialectical method.

For the first class of illustrations one may again turn to the problems which the spirit of that time furnished to the idealists. Whatever else the age of the Revolution and the following Napoleonic period were, they were such as to suggest that the dialectical, the antithetical, the contradictory occurrences in our thinking are founded on tendencies very deep in human nature. It was not the mere blundering of the individual men of those days which led to rapid and contradictory changes of popular opinion and of social action; for instance, the practical expression of the abstract doctrine of the rights of men led to a social situation in which the rights of the victims of the Terror were so ruthlessly sacrificed; the propaganda of universal human freedom was sustained by bloody wars; and in the end, the outcome of the Revolution was a military despotism. It is hardly a very deep account of these processes to say simply that the pendulum swings, and that excessive action leads to reaction. This is true. But it is a deeper truth that the ideas and passions of such a time are in their nature an union of antithetical tendencies. The passion for human liberty, in the form which it took during the early French Revolution was obviously an example of what Nietzsche has called the *Wille zur Macht*. Whatever the causes of the French Revolution, when it came it awakened a love of human freedom which was also a love of human might. The two aspects of this great fondness were antithetical, and for the moment inseparable. As the process developed they contended, and the one contradicted the other. How could one express one's regard for human freedom except through one's might? But might can be expressed only through finding some one to conquer. Conquest depends upon discipline; discipline requires a ruler.

Of course this obvious instance of the revolutionary tendencies awakened the reflections of our philosophers. But the instance did not stand alone. All the greater emotions are dialectical. The tragedies of the storm and stress period, and of the classical and romantic literature, are portrayals of this contradictory logic of passion. Faust asks the highest, and therefore contracts with the devil and destroys Margaret. The romantic poets so loved emotion that their works are mainly devoted to depicting the vanity of all the emotions. Outside of German literature, and in later times, one finds numerous instances of similar literary expressions of the dialectics of the emotions. The fascination and the power of Byron are due to his contradictions. Because of the loftiness of his emotional demands upon life, he finds only triviality and failure. His most characteristic ideal remains such a being as Manfred, whom the demons respect solely because his sins are deeper than theirs and because his internal remorse makes the external penalties of their hell seem by comparison insignificant. Manfred's poetic dignity consists in his absolute consciousness of his own moral worthlessness in all matters except his honest self-condemnation. Others are deluded into hope or fear. He knows that there is nothing to lose; and this makes him a hero. Instances of the dialectics of the emotions abound in the European literature of the period between 1770 and 1830. And not all such instances are tragic. There is a glory in winning all by abandoning all. Wilhelm Meister, like Saul, sets out to seek asses, and finds a kingdom. Or, as the classic lyric puts the cheerful aspect of this same dialectic:

> " Ich hab' mein' Sach' auf Nichts gestellt
> Und mein gehört die ganze Welt."

It is easy to say that all such phenomena express precisely the unreasonableness of the emotions. But a closer view shows that this dialectical tendency belongs rather to the active will than to the mere emotions. Upon this both Hegel and his bitter enemy Schopenhauer, though in very different ways, are agreed, and upon this they both insist. The mere sentimentalists amongst the romantic poets express such crises and such changes of point of view less effectively than do the more active natures. Byron is by nature a man of action who fails to find an absorbing career until he writes his last lyric after landing in Greece. That is why his utmost cynicism or his profoundest gloom has always a note of manliness about it that holds one's attention. To turn in the other direction, Goethe, full of emotional experience as he was, is rather a restlessly active man than a man of mere feeling. The dialectical process of his own activity brought him indeed to that splendid consciousness of calm and of inner self-possession which marked his best years; but his processes are always those not of the man of merely changing sentiments but rather of the man who became the controller of his fortunes, the master of his deeds.

Development through contradictions belongs then to the will, using that word in its merely popular sense, rather than to the relatively passive emotions. Can one still say that all such processes, whether of the emotions or of the will, belong *ipso facto* to the relatively irrational side of life? I will not at this moment answer this question upon its merits. It is enough for my present purpose to say that the idealists, whose position I am here merely illustrating, insist that this is not the case. They insist that the law of development through antitheses is characteristic not merely of the feelings, nor yet merely of what is unreasonable about our feelings and our will, but of the very life of reason itself. I have used the foregoing illustrations in order to show how deeply seated the dialectical or antithetical tendencies were in the life and in the literature of that age. The philosophy of our idealists was a reflection of the spirit of that time. Whether rightly or wrongly, these idealists did not seek to philosophize by merely purging their thoughts of all such antithetical tendencies, or by demonstrating that a sound thinker defines just one solid and stable truth such as enables you to ignore, once for all, every contradiction as a mere blunder. On the contrary, they developed a method which depends upon recognizing that the truth is a synthesis of antithetical moments or aspects, which does not ignore but unifies opposition.

This notion of truth is to many people so unsympathetic that I can only hope, at the moment, to indicate some way in which one who approaches it for the first time may be aided in treating fairly a point of view which only our later illustrations can render even tolerably articulate. One is tempted to say, "Fickle emotions we know, contradictory attitudes of will we know, but the hypothesis of an essentially antithetical constitution of rational truth is a self-confessed absurdity. Something must be true. What is true excludes what is not true. Antithesis may arise, through our ignorance and our hastiness, on the way towards truth. Conflicting hypotheses may even wisely be formed, weighed, tested, as a means to the discovery of truth. But an antithetical or dialectical constitution of the truth is logically impossible."

I will not here undertake to answer this objection. I am only trying to smooth the way towards an historical appreciation of this idealistic movement; so I may as well point out a motive which may help to make the dialectical method comprehensible to students of contemporary philosophy. Our idealists were, one and all, in a very genuine sense what people now call pragmatists. They were also, to be sure, absolutists; and nowadays absolutism is supposed to be peculiarly abhorrent to pragmatists. But of the historical, and perhaps also of the logical relations of pragmatism to absolutism we shall see more hereafter. What I now emphasize is that all these thinkers make much of the relation of truth to action, to practice, to the will. Nothing is true, for them, unless therein the sense, the purpose, the meaning of some active process is carried out, expressed, accomplished. Truth is not for these post-Kantian idealists something dead and settled apart from action. It is a construction, a process, an activity, a creation, an attainment. *Im Anfang war die That.* It is true, as I have said, that on the religious side these idealists had a certain sympathy with the tradition of the mystics whose God was found through an interior illumination. But I also said that the new doctrine was never meant to be any mere revival of mysticism. I tried to suggest its spirit by calling its religion a synthesis of mystical and of rationalistic motives. What I now add is that these rationalistic motives were dialectical, largely because of the stress that these thinkers laid upon the active element in thought, in truth, and in reality.

The connection between what I have called the pragmatism of these thinkers and their dialectical method was the same as the connection already indicated, in our illustrations of the general tendencies of the time, when we pointed out how the life of the will itself involves the presence of antitheses and of conflicting motives. If truth is what some active process finds, but finds only because this very activity itself creates the truth, then truth will not be something that you can merely describe in terms of monotonous consistency but will partake of the conflicting motives upon which the will depends. This thought lies very deep in the whole philosophy of this age. How this thought is expressed, our later illustrations will show.

LECTURE IV.

THE DIALECTICAL METHOD IN SCHELLING.

THOSE indications of the general nature of the dialectical or antithetical method of philosophizing with which the last lecture closed were intended to prepare us for a closer contact with the thinking processes characteristic of early post-Kantian idealism. Now I am to go on to some illustrations of this method, derived from the authors whom we are studying. My principal illustrations I shall choose, in this and in the next lecture, from one of the works of Schelling. Before doing so, however, I must consider a few preliminary and more general instances, in order to help us to a general view of the philosophical situation as our idealists found and defined it.

I.

So far in these discussions, we have insisted on two aspects of the post-Kantian idealism. The first aspect we defined by saying that while this whole movement of thought was indeed a product of the general spirit of that revolutionary and romantic age, the idealistic philosophy derives its principal technical problem from Kant's deduction of the categories. The problem thus set was that of the relation both of the form, and, in a certain sense, of the material data of human experience to the self and the selves whose experience this is. This general problem of the self, as we saw, inevitably involved the more special problems which concern the relations of the many human selves to one another, to the world of physical phenomena, and to the Absolute, as well as the connected problem of the mutual relation of the theoretical and the practical activities of the self. The second aspect of post-Kantian philosophy upon which we have dealt is the method of thinking which characterizes these inquirers. This was the antithetical or dialectical method. This method, as these thinkers employ it, is deliberately intended, not as a merely pedagogical device to lead an inquirer through preliminary errors to the final truth, but as a means of showing that the final truth itself is essentially dialetical or antithetical in its inmost constitution; so that you cannot utter a philosophical verity without giving it the form of an union or synthesis of explicitly opposed aspects or moments.

In order to suggest that so paradoxical a view of the nature of truth may after all possess a certain plausibility, I ventured in the last lecture to assert that our idealists were, upon the dialectical side of their thinking, essentially pragmatists, who regarded truth as always the outcome of a process or even as identical with a process, while the type of this process, to their minds, is that of our practical activity. And as I also suggested, the will, the practical activity of us all, is full of antithetical and so of dialectical characters. It is easy to illustrate this tendency empirically if you look at commonplace facts of active life. The will aims at contentment, yet in all active people it is restless in its tedium as soon as it reaches any stage of life where there is nothing to do. The will demands freedom from restraint, yet equally demands its expression in a social life which is full of restraints. It asserts itself in all sorts of self-surrendering, self-entangling, self-disappointing ways. The proud will of the vain man seeks with helpless dependence admirers and flatterers. The contrite will of the repentant sinner makes an ideal of despising itself, but may soon become, for that very reason, vain of its own humility, and then proudly wears, perhaps, a much prized professional ornament, the outward bearing or the dress that intrusively expresses to all beholders the fact of its self-effacement. The will of the people seeks freedom, and therefore accepts ere long the rule of despots or, in our age and land, the rule of the "bosses." Against such despots it in time revolts, and through this very revolt undertakes, not to obtain mere freedom, not the mere taking of a city by armed attack, but the hardest and most galling of all tasks, viz., the task of ruling the spirit, which the popular will, amongst us, has so far only partially learned to do. In brief, whatever the human will logically ought to be, it is in fact extremely prone to contradictions, not only on its lower but on its higher levels. When some men maintain that contradictory motives and deeds are naturally characteristic merely of womankind, this judgment only shows a lack of reflection. The antithetical expression of the will, viewed as a merely natural tendency, is neither manly nor womanly; it is human. Some people, to be sure, have, like Gladstone, more phrases than have others whereby to explain away their own natural contradictions of plan and of conduct. I intend no impertinence when I here add that the "strenuous life" even on its highest levels generally shows very marked and significant antitheses. This being the case, we saw, in the last lecture, that a philosophy which views the truth rather as something expressed in an active process than as a fixed realm of abstract principles or as a world of lifeless things in themselves, may be expected to make the most of the antithetical logic of the will in defining its own theory of the universe.

II.

Coming nearer to what is properly the foundation of the early idealistic philosophy, we may next point out that for these idealists, as already indicated, the self is to be the principle of philosophy. And the whole idealistic theory of self-consciousness turns upon the observation that the self is essentially a dialectical, an antithetical being, whose nature you can only conceive as an union of opposing, or as these thinkers often assert, of mutually contradictory tendencies.

This thesis was strongly suggested by Kant's deduction itself, although Kant avoids directly asserting it, owing to his elaborate training in holding his judgment suspended. He cannot tell what the self is. He refuses to commit himself upon the topic. Had he permitted himself to express more explicitly what his discussion implied, the antithetical character of the self would have come more fully to light. Let us consider some of the antitheses implied in Kant's deduction. All experience, according to Kant, is for the self, and receives its form from the active application of the categories of the self. Yet the entire material of experience—material without which these forms would be entirely empty—is not due to the self, but is a datum of sense, passively received, and so far is whatever it chances to be. Moreover, the self in our ordinary life as observers of nature is surely not conscious from moment to moment of the way in which this its own activity gives form to the matter of experience. If it were thus conscious of how its categories get into experience, the *Critique of Pure Reason* would be superfluous instruction. The self is primarily unconscious of even those most necessary deeds whereby it becomes an informing principle to which is due the form of all objective phenomena and their submission to intelligible laws. The self seems to us from moment to moment merely to find as datum what in truth is its own deed. Largely unconscious of its own life, then, is the self. Yet it is known to us, on the purely theoretical side, solely as the knower, as the subject of consciousness. Its first office is that of the knower; but its life is largely that of unconsciousness. Since experience is one, this subject of consciousness must be one. Another man's objective experience is indeed valid for me; nevertheless nothing appears to be more completely cut off and secreted from my knowledge than is any direct experience of what the contents of my neighbor's experience may be. We, the many men, are constructively one in our experience; yet, as phenomena, we are hopelessly apart, and our consciousnesses never flow into one. Finally, as we saw before, all human knowledge is of the empirical; yet the very conception of human experience is itself not an empirical concept. Nevertheless we are somehow to know that this concept has truth.

Meanwhile the self, as we just said, is known to us as the one knower of experience. But whatever we concretely know, becomes, by virtue of an application of categories to sense facts, an object of experience, a phenomenon somewhere in time and in space. So soon as we try to know the self, it also becomes one of the phenomena, an empirical ego, the mere "me" of ordinary life. This empirical ego, however, is simply not the true subject, the knower, whose unity of experience is a priori and necessary. For space, time, the categories—yes, all the world of phenomena, are in and of the self in so far as we are all the one subject. We—we as men, as various phenomena, as objects—are scattered about in our own forms of space and time, the prey of the natural laws that our transcendental unity of apperception predetermines. The self, as knower, categorizes all phenomena so that, for instance, the law of gravitation holds. Yet the empirical "me," the psycho-physical organism, falls, if that so chances, as helplessly out of the window as if his own understanding were not, according to Kant, the transcendental source of the form, and so of the laws, of all nature, including the laws which are exemplified by his own fall. Moreover, while the empirical ego is thus helplessly tumbling out of the phenomenal window, we may remark, regarding its correlate, the knower, that while that true self, the knower, *is*, we can speak of it in no objective terms, as a real fact, without applying categories to it; yet we know that such categories are inapplicable, since categories apply only to phenomena, and no phenomenon is the self that knows phenomena. Finally, the self is presupposed by us as a virtual or transcendental subject. Yet we can assign no final truth to the concept of the self regarding it as more than a merely virtual unity. And all these problems refer simply to the theoretical aspect of the case. The problems about the practical ego are left out of sight in this enumeration.

Thus the Kantian deduction introduces us to a richly dialectical realm. Nothing, of course, is easier than for one who listens to a sketch of these paradoxes to dispose of the whole subject, in his own mind, by simply saying, "What nonsense philosophers can utter," and then passing on to the order of his own day. That is indeed simple enough. Unfortunately one who thus disposes of the matter fails to note that he cannot attempt to articulate the common sense doctrines which bear upon these same topics of the self and its realm of knowledge without passing through a series of antithetical propositions which are quite as numerous and quite as paradoxical as those which Kant's deduction brings to the notice of a reflective mind. The difference between common sense and the philosophical doctrine is simply that the philosopher, by his finer analysis, reveals the paradoxes which our everyday consciousness veils by means of a more or less thoughtless traditional phraseology. The philosopher is more frank with his antitheses. He does not invent the paradoxes; he confesses them. Common sense pretends to be free from these contradictions; but its freedom consists in a mere refusal to reflect. The behavior of common sense much resembles that of the smooth-tongued and obtuse man, who confidently accuses womankind of a peculiar tendency to contradictions, without confessing that his own practical attitude towards all womankind is, as is usually the case, a very nest of somewhat portentous contradictions. As a fact, the problems of Kant's deduction are the problems of all of us. We all naturally insist that experience is our guide; yet we transcend our own literal experience with every assertion that we make, as for instance when we assert that other men exist and have experience. We all naturally regard ourselves and all our ideas, as a mere by-product of organic processes, and as the sport of physical fortunes; yet we persist that the real world is such as to be subjected, in some sense, to the laws of our reason, so that the more our insight possesses inner and reasonable clearness, the more it seems to us likely to be true beyond ourselves. In brief, we insist that the world is independent of our ideas; and yet we are always dealing, when we try to know, merely with a choice of the ideal attitudes of our own consciousness. To other men we frequently say, "The fact is thus and so, no matter what you think." And that seems to us the correct way of defining reality. But for ourselves we often say, "Since *I* cannot think it otherwise, it must be so." And that seems to us equally a correct expression of our relations to reality. Yet withal, we despise the philosophers for making this dialectic, and other such paradoxes explicit; and, like the obtuse man marvelling at the outspoken woman, we solemnly say to the philosopher, "Why *will* you thus contradict yourself?" In such cases, however, we are careful to tell neither the woman nor the philosopher what it is that we ourselves seriously believe. There are two simple ways to avoid all dialectical complications. One is an easy way, viz., not to think at all. The other is a prudent way, viz., not to confess your thoughts. Philosophers scorn both ways. They try to confess their contradictions, to live through them, and so, if may be, to get beyond them.

You will no doubt respond that the truth cannot consist merely of such contradictions as those indicated. The contradictions, you will say, must somehow be solved, reconciled, unified. When you become aware of this requirement, you emphasize a feature that the partisans of the dialectical method also kept in sight. To say that the truth is essentially dialectical is not, for them, to assert that the truth is a *mere* mass of contradictions—of accidental, hopeless and final conflicts. They have as much interest as anyone else in solving, in reconciling, in bringing to unity, the antitheses. What they mean by declaring that the truth is essentially antithetical or dialectical is, that contradictions such as those involved in the foregoing assertions about the self are not merely blunders due to inadvertence or to the incapacity of a philosopher, the hasty hypotheses of an ignorant learner, which have to be eliminated before one can see the truth. If the truth, for instance, involves, includes, determines, the process of self-consciousness, then the contradictory views of the self will express real moments, stages, features of this process—features of inner self-division and differentiation without which the self would not be what it is; so that you can only see what the final truth is by first grasping, and then bringing together into some higher unity, these antitheses; that is, by showing why the self must pass through these dialectical stages. How the unifying process of reconciliation takes place, if at all, according to these idealists, we are hereafter to see. The notable characteristic of the dialectical method which is here in mind consists in the thesis that you cannot grasp the truth of the self without taking account of these various mutually contradictory processes, so that nobody can say, "I have stated the truth about the self in a way that simply avoids all the contradictions of my predecessors (as for instance the contradictions of Kant), since these contradictions are mere blunders." No, in case the self is a process, and this process is, like that of the human will, one that essentially expresses itself in the assumption of mutually contradictory points of view, and only thereafter in some

higher synthesis of these, then the contradictions belong not to the blunders of the philosopher, but to the
very life of the self. When, in your account of the self
you assert contradictory propositions, no doubt your account is so far incomplete. You cannot rest in that account. You have not told the whole truth. But according
to the view of these philosophers, you cannot escape from
this incompleteness merely like the disorderly member of
Parliament, who says, at the speaker's order, "I with-
draw my assertion." Even the disorderly member does
not thus escape from his position. In effect he continues
to make the assertion thus formally withdrawn. If you
are to get the truth, the contradictions will prove to be
necessary moments in the expression of the whole truth,
even as the disorderly member's assertion and with-
drawal equally belong to and characterize his true position. You have gained by the contradictions if only you
first take them seriously and then attempt to rise above
them, for they are necessary stages of your self-expression.

III.

I have so far spoken of the idealists without discrimi-
nation. In historical sequence, they bore different relations to the dialectical method. Fichte, in the first
exposition of his *Science of Knowledge* was the first philosopher to define this procedure as the universal philosophical method. And he did so with explicit reference
to the fact that for him the self is the principle of
philosophy. The problem of the self is furnished by
the fact that whatever I know, whatever I acknowledge,
whatever I experience, I can only grasp the true meaning of my experience, of my assertions, of my insight,

by explicitly reflecting that all these contents are in
and of the self. That this self of philosophy is not the
individual man of ordinary life, appears from the very
outset of Fichte's discussion. The individual man of ordinary life is one of the beings to be defined by philosophy, and is certainly not the principle of philosophy.
The self, appearing at the outset as the abstract principle of philosophy, is to be transformed, by the philosophical process, into the true self, the self rightly
defined and embodied. The philosophical process in question is itself, at every step, one of reflection. Whatever
is asserted at any stage of the inquiry, one must forthwith add, "The self asserts this"; in other words, "This
is known as true in so far as *I posit this.*" The fact
I posit this is thus logically prior to the fact *This is.*
But hereupon one observes that the very problem of
philosophy, and in fact all the problems of life and
of science, may be summed up in the law that I always
inevitably posit data, of sense, of nature, and of life,
and posit them so that I view them as facts found
by me, but *not* posited by me. This then is my original
nature, viz., to acknowledge what I still stubbornly view
not as my acknowledgment, but as something *not* myself, and as given, from without, to myself. That this is
my nature, Fichte attempts to show, not merely upon
the basis of experience, but upon the basis of the observation that all logical classifications and discriminations
turn upon the recognition of what is essentially not myself. The fundamental paradox of philosophy is then
this, that, from the reflective or philosophical point of
view, I can know nothing which the self does not posit,
that is, define, acknowledge, determine, as its own object;
while, on the other hand, the way in which I, in real

life treat my world, is to view it as not myself, so that I posit my world precisely as that which I myself hold to be due to no act of mine. The first thesis of Fichte's philosophy is: The self posits just the self, and herewith posits whatever it can acknowledge as known or as knowable to the self. The equally inevitable antithesis is: The self posits a not-self; that is, defines its own object as not its own, but as another, opposed in nature to its own nature. The thesis and antithesis need to be united through a synthesis—a principle just to both these aspects of self-consciousness.

I shall not attempt to indicate, in this connection, how Fichte develops the synthesis thus abstractly defined. It turns out, in the sequel, that this thesis, as first formulated by Fichte, proves to be again dialectical, and to develop new antitheses, which require new syntheses. But the first form of Fichte's *Wissenschaftslehre* is peculiarly ill-adapted to a detailed treatment in a general discussion such as this. I have mentioned so much regarding its procedure in order to do a passing act of bare justice to the man who originated the modern dialectical method. Complete justice cannot here be done to Fichte. I pass on to another illustration of the dialectical method, appearing in a more highly developed form, in Schelling's *System des Transcendentalen Idealismus*.

Since our task is not one of a history of idealism, but only of illustrations, you will not object to my ignoring just now a great number of questions concerning this work such as your textbooks of the history of this period will readily answer. What Schelling's early relation to Fichte was; how close they were at one time together; but how Schelling's idealism from the first tended to contrast with that of Fichte—all these things are written in well-known books. I shall not expand upon such matters at present.

It is enough to remind you of the main contrast between Fichte and Schelling. Fichte was first of all an ethical idealist. To his mind the philosophical problem defined by the Kantian deduction of the categories was simply the problem how the self, not, mind you, the individual man, but the true self, whatever that may be, determines, consciously or unconsciously, the form and the matter of its own entire experience, expresses itself in the life of the individual man, and embodies its meaning in the process of its entire human world of action. The one key to the solution of the whole problem is, for Fichte, the ethical conception of the self. To live a life of action, and in this life to win nothing but its own full self-expression—this is the one purpose, the one principle of that self, which is itself the principle of all truth.

Action, however, as we saw, is essentially dialectical. It means winning one's own in a world which is all the while viewed as foreign. The active purpose posits its own opponent, and for that very reason views even this its own act of positing its opponent as an act forced upon it by an alien power. It thus defines its world in terms of an essentially incomprehensible antithesis, which makes action possible but which is never reducible to terms of a complete theoretical definiteness. The world problem can, therefore, be solved only in practical, in ethical, never in purely theoretical terms. If I merely saw my world as already my own completed work, I should have nothing to do. But I am essentially a doer. With the completion of all deeds, both I and my world would vanish together. To see my world as wholly mine is, therefore, simply the unattainable goal of an endless process. Theoretical philosophy can indeed define the categories, the forms of this process, but never its essential meaning. The meaning is that the world is the material for my duty, made manifest in my experience. Fortune, limitations, individual selfhood, social life, freedom, immortality—these are incidents in the endless undertaking. Experience seems foreign, just in order that our duty may be done in acts that win control over experience. Such, in the briefest outline, is Fichte's result.

Schelling, on the contrary, is only in the second place an ethical thinker. He is primarily devoted to theoretical construction. He is in fact a genius in the use of the speculative imagination. He is meanwhile an observer. He shares the typical restlessness of his age, the individualism, the self-confidence, and, in a measure, the romantic sentiment. But he is fond of nature, of art, and, in an amateurish way, of the detail of experience, and of intuitions. Despite his wonderful constructive skill, he is unfortunately a little too fond of fine phrases, and as a young man he is especially fond of a breathless rapidity of productive work. I have called him observant, and such he is, with a great keenness and sensitiveness to details; but he is not an investigator of experience, for whatever detail catches his attention at once awakens his fondness for fantastic analogies and for generalizations which express much more genius than discretion. The most orderly and finished of his early works is the *System of Transcendental Idealism,* where he had the guidance of Fichte as his predecessor, and the skill to supplement Fichte's one-sided moralism by a recognition of aspects of reality which appeal to the eye of the naturalist, and of the lover of art, rather than merely to the rugged ethical idealism of Fichte. Since I cannot attempt to give here any fair view of the wealth of Schelling's thought, I confine myself to this one book as an illustration of his methods.

IV.

For Schelling, at the time when he published, in 1797, the *System des Transcendentalen Idealismus,* the work of philosophy appeared to fall, as he tells us, into two distinct departments, eternally opposed, and therefore, as he adds, eternally inseparable. For the dialectic which the deduction of the categories suggests to him, is not only the dialectic of the self, but also the perfectly parallel dialectic of the not-self, or, as he usually calls it, of nature. The world of the deduction of the categories is, namely, on the one hand, the world as object, that is, as known; on the other hand the world as subject, that is, as the knower. Take experience as you find it. Abstract, by what Schelling regards as a deliberately one-sided but relatively justified abstraction, from the self that knows experience and from the problem as to how this self comes by its categories, and then you have before you the world called nature. This nature is of course not any "thing in itself." For the philosopher knows all the while that it is simply an object, and that the object implies the subject, so that what is known is known *to* somebody. But Schelling asks you first to be deliberately naïve, while you observe, although with the philosopher's thought in the background, outer nature; view nature as something found. Look not at the subject. Look without, at the object, at the totality of phenomena. At once, thinks Schelling, it then becomes obvious that nature itself, this endless phenomenon in time and space, is not a mere substance or a collection of substances, but is a process and a system of processes. An intuitive observation, an open eye, sees in nature the objective dialectic of the processes there present. Everything in nature, so Schelling insists, seeks its own opposite, and transcends, by its relationships, its own isolated being. We need not here pause to portray *how* this occurs. I will not trouble you with Schelling's philosophy of nature. It is enough to say that Schelling observed in nature three principal aspects: (1) On every level of nature there is a total relativity of the sort just indicated, whereby everything depends upon an antithetical relation to what is other than itself. Every natural object is an unity, or as Schelling likes to insist, a polarity, of mutually opposed tendencies, whose very opposition unites them. Attractive and repulsive forces as they exist in nature, the polarity of the structure of the magnet, the opposition of positive and of negative electricity, the general conceptions of chemical affinity as Schelling could then gather a crude notion of them from the then current investigations, the well-known unions of opposing processes in organic life, the facts regarding the reproduction of living forms—these were favorite instances of Schelling's general conception of the universally antithetical constitution of nature. I am not here estimating these views, only suggesting them. So much, then, for the total relativity of natural phenomena. Already, on this basis Schelling could, from his own point of view, draw the conclusion: Everything in objective nature has the same essential form as also appears in the life of the conscious self. Nature, viewed as object, appears thus as a community of unconscious, or as one might say, slumbering selves. The whole of nature has the structure of the life of the self.

(2) But now nature appears to us as a series of levels, or as Schelling calls them, *Potenzen*. On each level, the general forms of lower levels are repeated, but in a more complete and organized embodiment. The contrast between inorganic and organic nature is, for Schelling, an instance of such a contrast of levels or *Potenzen*. I need not here attempt to specify this doctrine as Schelling worked it out.

(3) Moreover, a general character reigns throughout nature which may be defined as a tendency towards the evolution of subjectivity, that is of mind. That which in us is self-consciousness, may be viewed, if we choose, in its psycho-physical relations. If this is done, self-consciousness appears in the natural world as a result of phenomenal conditions, and so as a product of nature. To the observer of the objective world, it is as if consciousness were an evolution from nature. And Schelling, who is fond of psycho-physical considerations, and who is a sort of halfway evolutionist, regards this point of view, for which consciousness is a product of nature, as, in its own way, perfectly justified. Begin thus with the object, and before your eyes it develops itself into a subject. If, as an idealist, you are all the while well aware that an object without a subject is impossible, so that you know, even while you thus observe the natural process, that nature is, for the knowing subject, its own phenomenon, you can nevertheless quite fearlessly admit that, so far as you deliberately abstract from the knower and merely look at the object as it appears, you then inevitably observe that psychic life is a product of a natural process. There is, in this way, a relatively justified materialism quite possible—yes, in its place inevitable for the philosopher. Mind is indeed, when thus

viewed, the outcome of nature. Schelling is sure that he can fully reconcile such a view with idealism.

What is, then, the result of all this deliberate abstraction, such as gives rise to the philosophy of nature? The answer is: Nature, as thus viewed, appears simply as a sort of external symbol or image of the self. Nature is the self taken as object—the self unconscious, hidden, but endlessly striving to free itself and to become conscious. Nature is the process whereby the dialectic of the self's own life appears in outward manifestation, first as dead mechanism, but never without an union of mutually opposing forces, then as the pervasive affinity that binds nature's oppositions together, higher still, as the life of plants and animals, and at length, as the natural process whereby the human individual becomes conscious. Thus, in outline, a philosophy of nature leads to an identification of the self with the natural process here presupposed.

Let us turn from this distinctly fanciful but profound interpretation of nature as, so to speak, the external apparition of an unconscious self, to the much less arbitrarily worked out, although still often wayward, constructions of the *System of Transcendental Idealism* itself.

V.

If nature is the unconscious form of the principle which becomes conscious in the self, and if, when we thus view the world, the conscious self phenomenally appears as an evolution from nature, how will the whole situation appear to us when we instead abstract, for the time, from all externally given data, and fix our attention wholly upon the subject, as that in and for whom

is all knowledge and all fact? Thus to view the situation
is, after one has learned the lesson of the Kantian deduction and of the idealistic movement, an inevitable philosophical undertaking. What Schelling wants to make
manifest is that, just as the objective view leads us to
regard nature as a process of unconscious dialectic out
of which, through a psycho-physical process, the consciousness of the self is evolved, so too this subjective
view of the same world will show us nature as that which
the self necessarily, although unconsciously, constructs.
Nature, viewed as the construction of the self, is the basis
upon which self-conscious activities are to be founded.
The Philosophy of Nature had asserted: If nature is, the
self must be evolved from it, for nature is an unconscious image of the self, struggling on various levels to
idealize its life into the form of self-consciousness. The
Philosophy of Transcendental Idealism will assert:
An experience of an external natural order is unconsciously constructed by the self, even as a basis for its
own attainment of self-consciousness. The categories of
this experience are to be deduced one by one, as the system develops. They are to be displayed as forms necessary to the attainment of conscious self-expression on the
part of the self.

In order to undertake the task thus set for the transcendental idealism, you have to form a philosophically
exact conception of the self. That in order to do this
you have to abstract from the empirical ego of ordinary
consciousness, we have already observed, and Schelling
explicitly insists upon this consideration. The human person whom I call myself, the "me," is one of the phenomena, or is a certain complex of phenomena. The self,
however, is just the *knower of phenomena*. If I am to

grasp the concept of this knower, of this subject as such, I must in some way be capable of a thinking process which, as Schelling also insists, "becomes immediately its own object;" and in the introduction to his *Transcendental Idealism*, Schelling enlarges at some length upon the conditions that must be fulfilled in order that such a thinking process should take place. We need not here enter into a discussion of these conditions. Certain it is, however, that the situation of one who undertakes, from any point of view, to *know the knower*, is a situation involving an obviously dialectical process. For, whatever object one seizes upon merely *as* object, whether that object be something in physical nature, or is some internal mental state, *this* object, as such, is certainly not the knowing subject, but exists for, or in relation to the subject. The self, then, is at all events not to be known as ordinary objects are known, for they are other than whoever it is that knows them. The self, however, in self-knowledge, is to be object *only* in so far as it is also self—known *only* in so far as it is also knower. It is to be fact for somebody only in so far as this somebody for whom the fact is, is identical with the very fact which is for him. Schelling therefore lays stress upon the thought that the self cannot be in its true nature sundered from the very act of self-consciousness. Its existence consists in this act. Its being is its own conscious doing. The self is no substance that could exist whether it were known or not. It exists only in so far as it is known, that is, only in so far as it is known to itself. "The ego is nothing different from its own thought; the thought of the self and the self are absolutely one," so Schelling states the case. The ego is *"kein Ding, keine Sache."* "It is object only `-- --` far as it makes itself object." Any purely *objective* existence then, must be denied to the self. It is not for any merely external being, but only for itself.

When one thus views the matter, one's first impression is that Schelling's philosophy of self-consciousness will turn out to be brief and in expression simple enough, but for that very reason hopelessly problematical. For a very few tautologies would apparently suffice to exhaust all that is possible in this account of a being who is to be only what he makes himself out to be, and just in so far as he knows himself, while he can apparently know of himself *only* this, viz., that he is just the knower. Such an autobiography appears so far to be tediously brief and uneventful. The paradoxical simplicity of such a doctrine is already sufficiently indicated if we remember certain Hindoo philosophers (of whom we now know a good deal, and of whom Schelling, at the time when he wrote this book, was almost entirely ignorant). These early Hindoo philosophers of the Upanishads, used to define the self by an endless abstraction from every sort and form of objective existence. What they obtained as the concept of the true self was therefore a certain pure emptiness of all contents. The self for them was said to be very lofty, but was as good as Nothing. Schelling's concept of the self seems at first sight to tend wholly in this direction of pure emptiness. "I am I" says the self; and so far this is the whole account of it.

It will be remembered, however, that for Schelling, the entire interest in this attempt to define the self is identical with that of Kant's deduction. The world of objects yonder—it is for me whatever *I* have to find in it; *therefore* my nature as knower is expressed in all this wide world that I know: this, as we have all along seen, is the thought upon which the investigations of all these philosophers are centered. When Schelling thus undertakes to define the self, he is therefore looking for what he himself calls the *Princip des Wissens.* He desires to show that this apparently empty concept of a being whose whole nature it is to exist as self-knower, is in fact an infinitely wealthy and fruitful concept. The act of self-knowledge, to be sure, *apparently* predetermines, so far as we can yet see, only itself. For if you attempt, in conception, to give to the self from without, an object—a content—that content by hypothesis is *not* the self, and therefore it is simply not the content of this still so mysterious act of self-knowledge. So long as the self is supposed merely to know such external ,contents, it is not knowing itself. On the other hand, if you deprive the self of all contents that are other than itself, that is, if you abstract from outer physical facts known, from inner feelings felt, from accidental happenings of fortune, and from all determined laws of its own mental nature; then what remains of the self but just nothing at all? Schelling nevertheless wishes to show that this apparently so empty concept is an adequate source of the whole system of truth.

His procedure in the development of this characteristic paradox of the dialectical method begins as follows: One has to distinguish, in any case, the two *aspects* of knowledge which the nature of the self, as thus defined, has somehow to unify. "If I be I, as I think I be," then as self-knower, I am in fact both object and subject, both known and knower, in one indivisible unity. But the two aspects of this unity are by definition as unsymmetrically related as they are inseparable. The self as knower, as subject, constitutes, by hypothesis, that aspect of this unity of subject and object which is the truer and the deeper aspect of the whole situation. For the character of the self as knower, is primal and fundamental. This whole idealism springs, as you remember, from the thesis that whatever object exists has to be viewed as existing for the knower—that is, as a fact for knowledge. The self then is above all a knower. Schelling calls this subjective side of the self its *ideal,* that is, its knowing, aspect. But viewed *merely* and abstractedly in this aspect, the self is, as we have now seen, limitless yet empty, without form, without contents—a knower, but so far a knower of nothing. On the other hand, by definition, the self is also to be knower of *itself.* That is, as *known,* the self has to be, by hypothesis, an object. Now, as Schelling hereupon says, an object is something determinate, something limited, bounded, distinguished from other objects, fixed by the attention, held fast, found. The self, precisely in so far as it is to be an object to itself, has, then, to include an objective aspect which is *not* boundless but which is definite and has form and is possessed of limits and distinctions. This is the subordinate, the secondary, the instrumental, and in so far the less true aspect of the self. Schelling calls it the *real* aspect of the self. This real aspect is never separable, except by abstraction, from the ideal one. The real aspect exists, so to speak, solely for the sake of the ideal aspect. It is as if the self said, "I am I; that is, I am the knower; but in order thus to be the knower I have, after all, to exist. In order to exist I have to have determinate content and character. I should not be the knower were I not also the known. And in order to be known I have to be found, felt, observed. And this I could not be unless I took on definite characters. So herewith I determine myself to become limited."

Thus the self, in order to be a self at all, is committed to an internal differentiation of its own nature, in such wise, however, that the differentiated aspects are not upon the same level. As knower, i.e., in its ideal aspect, the self is without determination of structure, since only objects are determinate. Hence, when viewed merely as knower, the self has no definite constitution. But as object known to itself, the self has a definite constitution; for only thus can it become object. It follows that, in general, no one objective form or constitution that the self can ever assume, can possibly be an adequate expression of its own ideal nature as knower. Yet, on the other hand, in order that the self should be known to itself, it must thus assume definite forms and constitutions. Its self-determined destiny is, then, to express itself in objective forms which are always inadequate to its own requirements. To adapt one of Mr. Bradley's phrases: Schelling's self might be said to have no assets except its objective embodiments; yet none of these are the whole of it, nor in any of them is its ideal aspect incorporated. So that were it only object, the self would be bankrupt.

To express the matter otherwise: Schelling regards the self as an union of two opposed activities, which are unsymmetrically correlated. The one is the limitless, in fact the illimitable, ideal, or the knowing activity. This no objective expression of the self ever exhausts. Whatever is known is not yet the knower. So in its knowing aspect, the self is nowhere simply expressed. The other aspect is the limited, the determinate, the definite, or the real activity. This expresses itself in single deeds, in determinate contents, in particular facts, in the explicitly finite constitution of experience. The forms of this finite constitution are the categories. The results of this activity of self-limitation are the phenomena of the world, as the subject knows them. These phenomena exist simply because, if the knower were not its own object, then the knower would not exist at all. Yet as they exist, these results of the objective activity are never adequate to their own purpose.

Were this the whole story of the life of the self, its dialectic process would simply consist of a life of inadequate self-expression in an infinity of known and self-constructed objects, no one of which would ever be the knower. But the process thus defined is not yet completely characterized.

It is not enough, thinks Schelling, for us to say that the self must thus be both a known object and a knowing subject and that it must possess as its actual constitution this union of mutually opposed activities. For in describing the self we have, after all, merely once more assigned to it a constitution. We have characterized it. We have treated it as a botanist treats a plant. We have thus not finished our own account. For that the self should *be* an union of these two correlative activities, this we can assert only by assigning to the self, by virtue of our very language, some objective character, as a sort of really existing natural fact. However, the self as knower must not only possess this constitution but must also know itself as possessing this constitution. That is, it must know itself as this indivisible union of a knowing subject (limitless, active, all-possessing, free), with a known object (determinate, self-opposing, limited, incorporated). That is, the self must view itself as thus internally divided, just as we are now trying to view it.

Hereupon there comes to light a consideration that

determines the form and the sequence of the parts of Schelling's *System of Transcendental Idealism.* This consideration is furnished by the difference between the conscious and the unconscious expression of the self.

The self, once more, is to be a self-knower. This requires, as we have seen, that the self should possess a dual constitution, that of the knower and that of the known. As knower it is formless, free from definite determination, limitless. As known, it is object, and hence determinate, full of definite distinctions, and, in every one of its expressions, limited, and thus inadequate to the limitlessness of its own true nature. All this, we have said, is its constitution. Now we add another reflection, "And this its own constitution," we say, "must become known to the self in order that it should be the self." Here, however, we define a new duality, namely, between the actual constitution of the self and the knowledge which the self possesses regarding this its own constitution. So far as the self possesses this constitution here defined but does not recognize that it possesses it as its own way of expressing itself, the self remains in a relatively unconscious position. It constructs, but observes the result of the construction as a fact, and not as its own inevitable self-expression. It so far regards its own constructions as if they were mere objects and not as if they were its own deeds. What it is all the while learning to know in these objects, is indeed its own work and nothing but its own work. Yet the self, on the lower level just defined, is unreflective. It so far does not recognize itself in these its own deeds. It *is* a subject-object. But it does not say, regarding its object, "This object I myself am." The inevitable asymmetry of the relation of object and subject necessitates, in Schelling's opinion, a stage of consciousness in which the self, in order to be its own object, expresses itself in a world of determinate phenomena, but still does not recognize that this is merely its own self-expression. In order, however, to be a self, our knower must express itself in this lower stage, and must in addition express itself in a still higher stage which it reaches when it not merely incorporates itself in a world, but recognizes itself in its own self-expression.

The result is so far this: The self must first unconsciously express itself in an endless variety of particular facts, in order that it should also be able, in a higher phase of its life, to recognize its own world as its own expression. Consequently, all conscious self-expression is based upon unconscious self-expression. The true self is indeed only as self-knower; but it cannot become self-knower unless it first expresses itself unconsciously, as it does in our consciousness of nature, and then expresses itself consciously, as it does in us when we are aware of our deeds as our own.

Thus it is that Schelling tries to make clear why the self, whose whole being it is simply to be self-knower, should nevertheless express itself in an endless variety of special experiences, while this very expression has to be made, at the outset, in a relatively unconscious form. The self, in giving itself embodiment, cannot recognize its own deed as its own unless it learns to recognize itself through a subsequent and distinct act of reflection. Thus then, self-consciousness is, for Schelling, rooted in a prior life of unconsciousness. I can only win the world for the self in case I first unconsciously express myself, in my natural life, and in my apparently foreign experience, and then reflect upon the expression. Self-attainment involves a prior search for the self, which first exists in an unconscious embodiment, and then and only then learns what is, after all, its essential art, namely that of self-conscious expression.

Such is our first glimpse of Schelling's position.

LECTURE V.

SCHELLING'S TRANSCENDENTAL
IDEALISM.

IN the latter portion of the foregoing lecture we made
our first acquaintance with Schelling's treatment of
the problem of the self, and also with his form of the
dialectical method. In opening the present discussion, we
shall be aided in recalling our result, if we endeavor to
make clear to ourselves what it was that Schelling supposed himself to have accomplished through the decidedly abstract and subtle considerations of which I sought
to give some sketch.

I.

The problem before him was, as we have seen, the problem of defining the relation of the objective world to the
self. At the outset of his treatise, he briefly sketched the
main considerations with which the result of the Kantian
deduction had already made us familiar. The world was
somehow to be defined as containing nothing essentially
external to the true self. The self that is in question is,
as we all along saw, not the self of any individual, but
the self that, at the outset of the system, expressly appears as an abstract principle of all knowledge and of
all reality. The objective world that was to be defined,
appeared at the outset as the realm of phenomena, that
is, expressly as the known, and as an object only in so
far as it is conceived to be known to the self. The self, on

the other hand, was defined as the knower. The problem
of this philosophy is, then, the one of defining the relation
of the known to the knower, of the object to the subject.
The problem appeared difficult for two reasons, opposed
yet correlative to each other. The first reason lay in the
fact that the knower, when defined with the degree of
abstraction that Schelling gave to the concept, tended to
appear as something which was simply not any object,
since an object is, *ipso facto,* something known and is
therefore not the knower of that object. The other difficulty of the doctrine lay in the fact that, granting the
knower to be somehow or other known, the concept of the
knower so far appeared to be a concept out of which
nothing would follow regarding the contents of the world
of phenomena. For whatever the knower is, Schelling
defines this being as in any case its own possessor, its
own activity. But the phenomenal world is certainly one
that we are not conscious of creating. We find it—this
phenomenal world—as something apparently independent of us, and as something that appears in consequence
incapable of being deduced from the nature of our own
consciousness. The ingenious discussion in which Schelling deals with this problem undertakes, as we saw, to
solve both aspects of the problem on the basis of a single
consideration. The self viewed as the knower is, so he
says, to be precisely the knower of itself, and consequently an object to itself. But the nature of an object,
so Schelling maintains, implies something finite, determined, and discovered or found. The nature of a subject,
that is, of a knower, implies freedom from determinate
character, since determination belongs to an object, and
consequently implies what Schelling calls a tendency to
transcend every limitation, or, as he prefers to say, an

endless or illimitable type of activity. The general sense of this thought is, that in so far as one is knower he lacks the limitations and determinations which characterize an object precisely because whatever is characterized as an object becomes thereby something determinate, and whatever one speaks of as determinate, or as having a definite nature, becomes thereby an object. In so far as the self is a knower, it must lack, then, such limitations and such determinateness. This purely abstract consideration could be supplemented by the fact that, as we are all aware, our effort to know always leads us, just so far as we are trying to be knowers, to strive beyond any particular limitations to which our knowledge is, so far, subject. If you view knowing pragmatically, that is, as a sort of voluntary activity, it is an essentially insatiable activity, which recognizes the presence of anything limited and determinate, only in order to strive beyond this by asking why, or by seeking for the origin of the given limitation—in brief, by accepting nothing determinate as final.

The essential characteristics of the subject and the object having been thus distinguished by Schelling, his whole undertaking in the work that we are sketching, depends upon insisting that the self is inevitably the synthesis of these two characters, the character of the subject and the character of the object. The doctrine thus suggested is interpreted by Schelling at every step pragmatically, that is, again, in terms of action and types of action. The self must know, therefore it must have an object for its knowledge. This object cannot come to it from without its own nature. That is the presupposition of the entire inquiry, and may for argument's sake be accepted. The object, then, must be due to the self's own nature. For in knowing, the self is simply to be dealing with itself. But the nature of the self as object is profoundly opposed to the nature of the self as subject. The activity whereby the self expresses itself in an objective way, is determinate and limited. But as knower the self expresses itself by casting down, transcending, overcoming determinations. Therefore the self must constantly act in a two-fold, and in a conflicting way. It must at once do what is necessary in order to present to itself objects that are found, that are therefore conditioned and determinate. It must also deal with these objects in terms of tendencies—to thought, to reflection, and to the discovery of relationships among objects; while these tendencies in their turn will always involve a striving towards the transcending of every given limit. Schelling, in the spirit of the dialectic method, expresses all this in the paradoxical way with which we have now become familiar. The self, as he insists, makes itself finite in order that it thereby may become and be infinite. In order to be limitless, it defines itself as limited. The general spirit of these paradoxes will, I think, be fairly comprehensible in the light of the foregoing. The whole affair has to be understood in terms of activity. In any case the self is a being of essential duality. In the well-known modern phrase, one might speak of it as a sort of dual personality, one of whose modes of activity is essentially opposed to the other. The subjective activity, the activity of the knower as knower, is devoted to completeness, and to the attainment of a limitless self-possession; while the activity of the objective or known aspect of the self, is devoted to restraints, limitations, determination, and finitude in general. If we call these two aspects of the self the real and the ideal aspects, then the real aspect is the fact-maker, the ideal aspect is one which constantly rises above mere facts, either idealizing them through its thought, as our industrial arts and our sciences do, or undertaking in a philosophical interpretation to view the fact-making process as its own expression and embodiment.

So far, then, Schelling has insisted upon a principle which from his point of view tends to define why the world endlessly appears to our consciousness not as the self but as something else. The knowing process appears to us to be in sharp contrast to the existence of the facts known. We are right, according to Schelling, in recognizing this duality. We are wrong in missing the unity that lies beneath the whole affair. This unity can only be understood from the side of the knower. If we view the facts as existing merely because they are required by the activity of the knower, and if we view the knower as a synthesis of two tendencies which are in an essentially unsymmetrical relation to each other, so that whatever the one tendency demands the other at every point directly opposes, then we shall have made a beginning of comprehending, according to Schelling, the situation of the self.

II.

But herewith only one aspect, and by no means the most fruitful one, of Schelling's use of the dialectical method, comes into sight. The various stages in which, in his doctrine, the life of the self appears, are determined by another principle than this primal duality. This other principle is what one might call the principle of reflection. It is implied, to be sure, in the very conditions that the principle of the duality of the self has just expressed. Whatever the self is, that in its wholeness it

must reflectively know itself to be. The definition of the
self implies that, however unconscious it may prove to
be in any of its special expressions, in its absolute wholeness it possesses no character that is not again known to
the self. When Schelling insists upon this fact, a new
and higher duality in the nature of the self is thereby
revealed. The self, as we have just seen, possesses what
one might call its primal duality, the contrast of its objective and subjective aspects. It possesses upon any
stage of its expression what one might further call its
secondary or derived duality—namely, the duality of
its expression, and of its reflection. It is indeed one thing
for the self to possess any activity, or internal conflict,
or variety, or contrast of aspect; it is quite another for
the self to be conscious of this, its own condition, variety, or complexity of manifestation. Schelling consequently insists that since the expression of itself, and its
consciousness of this expression, are two-fold, and since
the consciousness of a given form of expression must
depend upon the objective presence of this form within
the life of the self, therefore the self must necessarily
have an unconscious life, an unconscious mode of self-
expression, in order to possess a conscious life and a
conscious self-expression. In other words, to say that the
complete self is completely conscious, inevitably implies
that the self is also, in its first expression, unconscious.
As Schelling states the case, "Whoever is unable to see
in every activity of the mind the unconscious element,
whoever recognizes no region outside of consciousness
as belonging to the self, will be wholly unable to comprehend either how the intelligent activity of the self
forgets itself in its product or how the artist can become completely lost in his work. For such a person, who

ignores the unconscious aspect of the self, there exists no creative activity but ordinary moral activity; and such a person is incapable of seeing how necessity and freedom can be unified in the act of creation.''

This reference to artistic activity furnishes an illustration in terms of which, whether one agrees with Schelling or not, one can understand how he is viewing the life of the self. The self is indeed a knower. But prior to every knowledge is an unconscious possession of the object. Knowing is a reflecting upon one's own unconscious creations. Without unconscious activity, no conscious activity. Such a character of consciousness is especially furnished by the work of genius. The work of genius is unconscious in origin, determining for that very reason the richer and more surprising consciousness, when it is once produced. And so here is the place to remark once for all that the self for Schelling is essentially of the type of a productive genius. It produces unconsciously, in order that it shall furnish itself with material for consciousness. Hence, it always meets its own products as apparently foreign facts. Its world is its own deed; but it is essential to the process of self-consciousness, that the self should first fail to recognize the world as its own deed, and should therefore at the outset find it as something external to itself, even in order to have the opportunities to win through the comprehending, the conquering, and the possessing of this world, its own attainments of self-consciousness.

III.

On the basis of the principles thus reviewed, Schelling feels warranted in defining a series of expressions of the self which, at the close of the book under consideration, he himself recapitulates. I here follow and also expand this summary. In the first place the self, that is, not the individual self but the self as principle, of knowledge and of being, expresses itself through its objective activity, and becomes aware of this expression dimly and imperfectly, in the form of immediate experience, of sensation, of the simple consciousness that something is. The self of immediate experience finds countless facts. By what is essentially a single act of self-determination it presents to itself a limitless realm of contents, every one of which, as first found, appears at this stage entirely foreign. Limitless this world of facts must be, for no single object of immediate experience, no one group of sensations would suffice to express the whole self, in so far as it is the knower. Foreign every one of these facts must seem to the self, in so far as it is knower, just because the facts are due to the before-mentioned objective activity of the self, which, as we know, is opposed to its subjective activity by virtue of the primal duality. Not only must these sensations appear foreign to the self; the philosopher also recognizes that in their detail they must remain endlessly beyond any philosophical deduction. Their existence, indeed, is something which for the philosopher is an a priori necessity. For the self is, and the self therefore must possess its objective activity. But in this primal form the objective activity must be as arbitrary as it is limitless; and it is an entire blunder to suppose that Schelling imagined the detail of immediate experience to be deducible a priori. What is here to his mind deducible a priori is just this primal existence of an opaque and immediate infinite wealth of data.

But it is of the nature of the self to recognize the contrast between its ideal and real aspect. The steps by which, in Schelling's account, the self comes to do this, need not be further characterized in this summary. It is enough to say that, as observer of the given facts, the self expresses its ideal activity in a fashion which includes these categories which Kant had ascribed to the intelligence. These categories, belong, I say, to the other, to the ideal aspect of the self's activity. Like the Kantian categories they come into synthesis with immediate experience, and the result of this synthesis of real and ideal is the world not of immediate experiences but of intelligible, phenomenal objects. This is the world of our experience of nature. Here the contrast between the objective and the ideal aspects of the self still remains. It also remains true that upon this stage, despite the synthesis, the self is conscious of its objects, but not of its own deeds, in so far as they are mere deeds. It finds the products of its activity; it cannot recognize them as merely its own products. Therefore it inevitably views them as natural phenomena subject to law. This lawful aspect of the facts is, to be sure, determined after the Kantian fashion, by the ideal aspect of the activity of the self. The phenomena are therefore subject to rational law. They are not, like the immediate experiences, *merely* found. They are viewed as constructions, but as constructions due to a process of whose nature the self is unconscious. Nature presents the intelligible facts to the experience of the self. The self recognizes the intelligence thus present in nature; but it views this intelligence as a phenomenal, and in so far unexplained fact. Were the self to remain upon this level, it would remain eternally unconscious of its genuine ideal activity. It would not know itself with any completeness. It would simply construct like a god, but, unconscious of its divinity, would observe like a child.

If we view this stage of the expression of the self, there is still another aspect to be considered. The true self, as we saw, is not any individual ego. But its objective world, as now defined, does indeed contain individual empirical selves. It does so, because amongst the objective facts of which the self, on this stage of its manifestation, is conscious, is the fact of the contrast between the intelligent finding and understanding of facts on the one hand, and the existence of the intelligible phenomena on the other. In other words, at this stage the self is not only aware that these phenomena are found, but it is also aware that somebody, an observing empirical subject, finds them, inquires into them, thinks of them, and in so far knows them. In brief, the duality of the real and ideal self is, upon this stage, presented as being in itself merely a portion of the realm of phenomenal facts. Thus the empirical ego, the self as individual, is indeed one of the facts found amongst the other phenomena. As this empirical self, by virtue of the process whereby it comes to be observed is found as limited by an infinite realm of other facts, Schelling endeavors to show that the empirical ego must appear in the realm of experience as limited to a special and incomprehensible fortune, which in space and time is bound to this place and this age. The empirical ego, then, as one of the phenomena, is as limited as any other of the determinate facts of the universe. It is not completely self-possessed. It is the creature of nature and of destiny. It is wholly subject to fortune. It is unconscious of its origin, and can understand this origin only in terms of what it can make out from studying the laws of nature.

IV.

The whole self, however, in order to be the whole self, cannot remain upon this unconscious level. On the other hand, this stage of acceptance of facts without consciousness of their ideal source, is indeed an internally complete phase of combined consciousness and unconsciousness. Schelling, as you see, believes that he can understand why the complete self must appear on this stage, which is essentially the stage defined by the Kantian deduction of the categories. He is also sure that nothing that can occur upon this level furnishes any reason why the intelligence should pass beyond it to a higher level of consciousness, while, on the other hand, the nature of the true self essentially demands that this stage of consciousness should be transcended. To what tendency of the self, then, is due the power to reach a stage of reflection higher than the one just defined?

Hereupon in his development of his doctrine Schelling lays stress upon a consideration which Fichte had already developed in those of his early works in which he deals with ethical problems. That stage of reflection in which the self becomes able, not merely to understand the intelligible character of phenomena, but to view its deeds as its own, and so to make a beginning in comprehending its ideal activities, is attainable only through a *social consciousness.* Left to itself, without a variety of inter-related selves, as an essential part of its life, the pure self would be intelligent but unconscious of the source of its intelligence. True self-consciousness, that is consciousness in which the relations of the subjective and objective activities become explicit is possible only for a social being. This thought, momentous for the whole later development of idealism, is emphasized by Schell-

ing at a critical stage of the work which we are considering in a very interesting manner. The possibility that
the self should express itself in the variety of individual
forms is suggested by that view of the nature of individuality which I have just very summarily indicated.
In observing its world of phenomena, the self observes
its own ideal activities as themselves phenomena only
in so far as these activities are concerned with the observing, the finding, the knowing of objects. That is, the
empirical ego is first known merely as the knower of a
foreign world, to which he comes as the intelligent onlooker. But that the empirical ego is an expression of the
very activity to which the whole world of phenomena is
due, this fact cannot become explicit for the self, in so
far as the self remains upon the stage of an intelligent
observation of phenomena. The empirical ego is, however,
as we saw, an observer of fragmentary and determinate
sets of phenomenal facts, appears on the scene at a particular point of space and time, is like any other phenomenal fact, due to an incomprehensible limitation, and
is immersed in an infinite realm of natural facts, to
whose laws his own fortunes are subject. Individuality
therefore appears in indefinitely numerous and various
natural forms. None of these forms completely display
what the self is. And in so far as they are phenomena,
none of these individual and empirical ego-phenomena
can display the true activity of the self.

But all these finite selves are also possessed of
the truly ideal, of the genuinely constructive subjective activity of the self. Yet in no one of them can this
activity be observed as a phenomenon. In each of them
it is present merely as the essence of their individual
will, as the constructive principle that determines their

lives. But now, as Schelling insists, when these selves come into mutual contact, when the act of one, becomes a significant fact for the other, each of these expressions of the self wins from the contact an entirely new, a social sense, of the meaning of his own nature. I become aware of my own activity as mine only by virtue of the fact that my activity is in some respect limited or hindered by what I recognize as the act of another self. In other words, the higher reflection which characterizes the moral being, the reflection which enables one to say this is my deed, is a reflection made possible only by the mutual relations of various selves. The sense of this doctrine, which Schelling derived from Fichte, and which he here expresses with great definiteness, is the same as that which with reference to recent investigations Professor J. M. Baldwin and I have emphasized, each in his own way, as a matter of the empirical psychology of self-consciousness. One cannot say that Schelling's account does very much to rid the process described by him of its distinctly empirical appearance. As a fact, a reflective self-consciousness is always accompanied by the recognition of others than myself. I acknowledge another self beside me, and in doing so I become aware of myself. Schelling insists upon this point. He attempts to show, in the way just indicated, that a variety of individual selfhood actually belongs to the modes of self-expression which the self finds in its world. But the recognition of one individual by another individual appears in his account as an irreducible fact. This fact is in general necessitated by the requirement that the self should come to consciousness of its own activity. And such consciousness actually occurs in no other way. Self-consciousness, as, in agreement with Professor J. M.

Baldwin, I have stated the case, is what one might call a social contrast effect. You know yourself by contrast with the other man, or by contrast with many other men, with God, or with your own ideal self. And we learn self-consciousness through our social relations. It is at all events characteristic of the idealism whose fortunes we are following, to lay great stress upon this essential feature of the reflective self-consciousness. In the large perspective of Schelling's doctrine of the self, the stage of consciousness which he calls intelligence, and which we have reviewed in the foregoing, has been characterized by profound unconsciousness of its own active character. Intelligence observes, observes the world of immediate experiences, and of intelligible law. It categorizes. It defines. It actually sees itself in all it sees; but it sees itself as foreign, as nature, as phenomena. To be sure it in one respect goes further than this. Since this, its whole intelligent life, after all depends upon the conflict of real and ideal activities, and since the ideal activity, the constructions of the intelligence, are everywhere limited, determined, by the phenomena, the intelligence observes itself as present under the form of empirical individuality, bound to an organic life, limited to this or to that part of the world. And in so far the intelligence is indeed psychological in its interests. It observes mental phenomena, and in so far it inevitably observes various empirical egoes, various individual types of experience. But in all this intelligence does not know that it is observing its own constructive activity. In the social life, and only in the social life, however, does the self awaken to the reflection that its deeds are its own; that is, that its ideals are the source of objects, are productive of facts.

With the reflective process which thus becomes possible, the self begins to be aware of what it is, namely, a creator. Its knowing becomes for it also a constructive activity, a creative principle. With this it is indeed at first remote enough from knowing itself to be the creative principle of its whole world. Its constructive or ideal activity now comes to its consciousness only at first in the form of the deeds of one individual over against other individuals. It enters the practical world where action rather than the intelligent comprehension of facts forms the central interest. But herewith the immediate result is, of course, not the reduction of its world to unity, nor the complete recognition of its own unity as a world creator, but an increase of variety. The various individual selves of the practical world are primarily subjects and not objects, ideal beings rather than phenomena, self-determining rather than determinate, free rather than subject to law. But on the other hand they are bound together, they are inter-related by the fact that they possess the realm of intelligence in common. They are many in so far as they are also able to act upon one another, for through their interaction they are able to recognize each other's existence. And their interaction implies a recognition of common subjects, that is, a recognition that the same world of phenomena is common to them all. The world of phenomena thus gets a renewed, an increased grade of objectivity. One of the principal reasons why common sense generally refuses to view phenomena merely as objects for a subject, is that since phenomena are common to all the various intelligent subjects, they appear independent of any one individual subject, and so are taken to be real, apart from knowledge. As Schelling puts it, the world of the intelligence becomes for the first time a real world in so far as it exists for the many subjects. The presupposition for every concrete activity of the subjects is therefore this, that their acts should conform to the laws of nature. Whatever they do belongs also to the realm of phenomena. Since they are also aware of their deeds as their own, they thus become conscious of a certain preestablished harmony between nature and the human will. But this preëstablished harmony is itself something subject to determinate limitations. Human freedom is possible only in particular deeds at certain times, in particular places. Every man's activity is limited. Every deed of an individual presupposes the whole objective world process in which he finds his own phenomenal place. The position of the free agents is therefore essentially paradoxical. They express the deeper, the ideal aspects of the self. But they do this in a way which makes every one of their deeds appear as a mere incident in the world process, and as an expression of a human nature whose natural causation can only be defined by referring it for its source to the whole of the past history of the world.

However, reflection once established, the ideal activities of the free agents become themselves the topic of mutual criticism and of self-estimate. The moral consciousness arises and defines the ideal of the ideals, the principle according to which all ideal activity ought to be guided. And this is the principle of the complete and free expression of the selves, as the life of one self. Thus at last the ideal principle of the self comes in its unity before consciousness. And thus the contrast between free expression of the self as subject, and the natural limitations of human nature as the objective aspect of the life of the self, becomes a central fact. Hereupon Schelling tells us that it is this fact which forms the topic and the interest of universal history. The history of humanity is the tale of the contest between fortune and free will, and on the other hand between the caprice of the individual and the destiny of humanity. The problem of history in its most general form is this. The ideal activities of free agents constitute in their unity the only expression that the ideal activity of the self can ever consciously get. In so far as the ideal activity of the self expressed itself simply in the construction of natural phenomena, it was unconscious. It comes to consciousness only in human beings, and in them only in so far as they are aware of their free choice in their coöperation and in their conflicts with other human beings. But since the ideal activity of the self is to be completely expressed in the world of life as a whole, it must be the destiny of the world to unite somehow the necessity that the ideal should be wholly realized, and should be realized in the entire course of human history as a whole—to reconcile this necessity, I say, with the fact that the only expression which the ideal can ever attain, is its expression through the free choices of individuals—choices which, as free, need not be ideal at all in any but the capricious sense of the momentary and perhaps wayward deed.

V.

Thus then, for Schelling, the world problem, which at the outset of his discussion was merely the problem as to how the self is related to its world of experience, now becomes the problem which is determined by three factors: (1) the natural process of the phenomenal world, (2) the free will process of individuals, (3) the ethical or absolute ideal, which in demanding that the self should be completely expressed, and expressed in conscious form, demands that the natural destiny of humanity should in the long run so overrule the individual caprices, that an ideal result of history, an ideal evolution of the ideal, should be the net result of the life struggle of humanity. The problem once thus stated, Schelling in a decidedly dramatic climax of his discussion, solves it by two considerations, taking him into regions quite remote from the philosophy of Fichte. You will remember that, at the outset of our account of Schelling, during the last lecture, we first met the self in a problematic guise, which for the moment threatened to result in the total failure of our enterprise to become anything but a thought of Hindoo mysticism. The self as knower was to be simply identical with its own object. Until we observed with Schelling the unsymmetrical relation between the objective and the subjective activities, we could see for the moment no way out of the empty phraseology of the assertion, "I am I." The self appeared to be complete at the instant when, being its own empty object, it was nothing at all. But in any case the self then appears to us as a certain identity, whose nature is so far undefinable. Having carried his investigation through such elaborate complications, having distinguished conscious and unconscious activity, having so sharply distinguished object and subject, individual consciousness and true self, ideal and real aspects, intelligence and free will, nature and society, humanity, the destiny of humanity, and the ideal of humanity, Schelling now suddenly and in characteristic fashion returns from all these varieties to an assertion of the original identity of the self with the self, of the objective with the subjective, as not only the beginning, but also the

end of the entire undertaking. The principle which we
have been calling the self, is a principle so far of self-
differentiation. We are now reminded that the unconscious and the conscious natures of this self are essentially identical, that the self, although endlessly individual, has also been, throughout this process, essentially
impersonal, indifferent to every one of its own distinctions, except as this distinction should be of use in illustrating its own identity and self-possession of nature.
All then is the self; but the self, what is the principle
at the very heart of its nature? Schelling again replies,
*"The identity of its conscious and unconscious proc-
esses."* This identity does indeed demand a variety; in
fact all the varieties that we have been following. But
the identity requires these varieties merely as its form
of appearance. It is by itself deeper than all the varieties.
The identity, then, of conscious and of unconscious
processes, of objective and of subjective expressions, of
real and of ideal activities, of the world and of the goal
of the world, of humanity and of the destiny of humanity
and of the purpose of humanity, this identity is after
all not only what we have presupposed, but as Schelling
insists, it is what we have necessarily found as including, demanding, and unifying all these varieties. The
Identity, then, may well be called the "Absolute;" and
Schelling hereupon so calls it. The Absolute is precisely
that which the self throughout the whole development
has been trying to be. The Absolute is, as Schelling now
paradoxically maintains, neither the subject nor the object, but essentially, as he puts it, the "Indifference," or
as one might better say, the essential unity of both. Its
form is that of subject over against object, of pursuit
over against ideal, of deed over against fact, of attain-

ment over against finitude and conflict. But in itself it is rather the center toward which all these differences point. Its root is in unconsciousness, its flower is in human effort. Its nature completely unites and identifies conscious and unconscious principle.

A certain illustration and aid in interpreting this somewhat obscure doctrine is furnished by one more feature which Schelling introduces at the close of his discussion. The highest apparition of the Absolute, apart from philosophical reflection, is, he tells us, not nature, not man, not moral activity, not human history, but art, and its producer, namely, genius. An artistic genius is the nearest to the complete incarnation of the Absolute that we can expect to find. Art is the fullest expression of the absolute identity of conscious and unconscious activity that our experience furnishes. In the work of art we find that whose origin lies deep hidden in the unconscious. But it expresses a meaning, when it is of the highest artistic type, which an infinity of conscious activity would be needed to exhaust. The work of art is a perfect synthesis of objective production, with subjective significance. It is a product of nature, namely of the nature of the artist, and so it is in perfect harmony with the entire nature of things. In consequence, it has all the characters which the intelligence has found in the rational order of the phenomenal world. On the one hand, it has ideal values, that is, it stands in such relation to our present conscious activity as the moral ideal stands, for it is the goal of an endless attainment. On the other, it is the ideal present, completely embodied, finished, found. Thus it brings before us, as completely as may be, the identity, the unity, of all the various elements which experience and action, science and life, subject and ob-

ject divide. We have sought, then, the self; we have
found the Absolute; and the best incarnation of the
Absolute is art.

Such is an outline of this distinctly romantic and
frequently fantastic work of Schelling's genius, a work
which Schelling himself could not well regard as final,
and which I have thus expounded not because it is my
purpose in this course to discuss either the evolution or
the later forms of Schelling's philosophy but because we
find herein the illustration of very notable motives of
this whole idealistic movement.

LECTURE VI.

HEGEL'S *PHAENOMENOLOGIE DES GEISTES.*

I.

IN my series of illustrations of the early idealism I now come to a work which is in many ways the most remarkable production of German philosophy between 1790 and 1810.

The *Phaenomenologie des Geistes,* despite its close relations to the general movement of thought at the time, contains a degree of originality both of conception and of execution, which sets it above any single work either of Fichte or of Schelling. In the series of its author's productions, it again stands in a very marked place, being distinctly the most original and individual of all Hegel's works. And, despite its notoriously barbarous style, which has made it the horror of the recent German historians of literature, it has very close and important relations to the literary movement of the time; and were it composed in a language which ordinary students of literature could comprehend, it would undoubtedly occupy a very notable place in the annals of the literature of the romantic period. As the product of Hegel's early manhood it has a greater freedom of imagination and of constructive power than belongs to his later works. In its comments upon political and social problems, it shows indeed the personal temperament which always remained characteristic of Hegel, but it lacks the somewhat pedan-

tic political conservatism which marks the treatises of the
last decade of Hegel's life, composed when he was professor at Berlin, during what has been called by his enemies,
his "bureaucratic" period. Because it has become customary for the modern historians of philosophy to judge
Hegel by his later works, and because the political conservatism of his Berlin period and the dictatorial manner
that he then assumed rendered him unpopular to the
generation of German liberals whose influence culmi-
nated in the year 1848, the *Phaenomenologie* has remained unduly neglected. Few of the textbooks of the
history of philosophy give it much more than a per-
functory summary. Haym in his book *Hegel und Seine
Zeit* discusses the work, but with an austere lack of
sympathy for what was most characteristic about it.
Windelband in his *History of Modern Philosophy* speaks
of it much more sympathetically, but characterizes it, not
altogether unjustly, as the most difficult treatise in the
history of philosophy. Difficult the *Phaenomenologie*
certainly is, even if one comes to it in the right spirit.
The customary aversion to the work has, however, been
partly due to a failure to consider it in the right relation
to the literary and social background characteristic of
the time when it was produced. In only a few instances,
so far as I know, have the critics of the German literature
of that time seen the interest that attaches to the *Phaenomenologie* from the purely literary side. Of all the brief
summaries of the book in the histories of philosophy, the
sketch which Zeller gives in his *Geschichte der Deutschen
Philosophie seit Leibnitz* is to my mind the best. The
account of Rosenkranz in his *Life of Hegel* is decidedly
valuable, although I feel that Rosenkranz himself regards
the book a little too much from the point of view of its

relation to Hegel's later system. It ought, I think, rather to be taken first of all as an expression of a very remarkable stage in the development of German idealism; it ought to be viewed as what it is, a very marvelous union of a rigid technical method of analysis of problems on the one hand, with a remarkably free use of literary imagination and historical comments upon the other. This union is such as to make the work of distinctly unstable value for systematic philosophy. The critic who expects to find logical formulations and metaphysical doctrines, and who in fact finds many such in the book, is misled in his judgment concerning those portions of the work where Hegel indulges in the portrayal of more or less idealized characterizations of historical types, of individuals, and of social movements. As these characterizations have a relation to the logical and metaphysical doctrines which is not at first sight easy to understand, the critic is likely to find these passages of character study simply incomprehensible, or to regard them as wayward interruptions of the logical development, or even, worst of all, as absurd efforts on Hegel's part to deduce a priori the history of man, and the psychological development of human character, from the categories of his system. On the other hand, the student who turns to the book with the interest of the historian of literature, is terrified by the technical vocabulary, by the strange array of categories, by the evidences that the whole is intended to illustrate, and in some way to prove, some system regarding the universe. If the *Phaenomenologie* be viewed, therefore, with reference to the announced purpose of the author, which is to furnish an introduction to his forthcoming system of philosophy, the work must certainly be called a failure. Few or none of its contemporary read-

ers could have foreseen what was to be the outcome of
the doctrines regarding the real world which were indicated in his introduction. Few would have felt themselves introduced to anything. For it is indeed true that
the technical aspect of the work needs considerable explanation in the light of Hegel's later work. On the other
hand, nobody amongst Hegel's contemporaries could
have been much enlightened by the untechnical portions
of the work, because these were embedded in the obscure
vocabulary and in the suggestions of the metaphysical
doctrines.

Despite all these things, when once we undertake to
consider the *Phaenomenologie* upon its own presuppositions, we discover a great deal that remains permanently
interesting. The interest is of two sorts. In the first place
the *Phaenomenologie* is a study of human nature, as it is
expressed in various individual and social types. From
this point of view the title which William James has
employed for his book, *The Varieties of Religious Experience,* could well be adapted to characterize Hegel's
treatise. It is so far a book describing, in serial order,
some varieties of experience which, in Hegel's opinion,
are at once characteristic of the general evolution of
higher mental life, and are examples of the transition
from common sense naïveté to philosophical reflection and to the threshold of an idealistic system. The
choice of these varieties of experience, of these types of
character, and of social development, is for us today
somewhat arbitrary. There can be no doubt that this
choice is distinctly due to the state of politics and of literature and of European life generally in the years
when Hegel wrote this book, namely in the time just before the battle of Jena. Had Hegel written it at the close

of his career, during the time of the political reaction which preceded 1830, he would unquestionably have chosen a different group of types. Yet there is no doubt that the human types which he actually portrays in the work are significant, are characteristic of great problems both of personal life and of society, and despite the somewhat arbitrary array in which Hegel presents these types, and despite the extremely severe criticism to which he frequently subjects them, the work done is of permanent importance and interest. In the second place, the interest of the book is in part truly philosophical. It does not fulfil its purpose of easily introducing the learner to a philosophical idealism, but it contains a very thoroughgoing application of the dialectical method, and a very important series of reflections on the problems of idealistic thought.

My own present effort to give some hints of the contents of the *Phaenomenologie*, will endeavor to be just to both these interests. The actual waywardness with which Hegel combines metaphysical analysis and free portrayal of types of human character, the unquestionable difficulty of the whole discussion, the unsatisfactoriness of the entire argument, viewed as a systematic presentation of idealistic doctrines, the arbitrariness of this singular union of imaginative construction, psychological portrayal, and metaphysical reasoning—all this I shall recognize; and yet I shall try to indicate how significant the book is, when rightly taken. In order to view it fairly, you have to treat it, I think, as a whole genus of highly original literary and speculative works and authors should be treated. It is with the *Phaenomenologie* as it is with Schopenhauer, with Nietzsche, with Walt Whitman, with Browning. In dealing with such original and occasionally crabbed instances of genius, people are far too often divided into the blind followers who worship the master or his book, because of the eccentricities of both, and the blind opponents who can see nothing but barbarism or waywardness, because this type of genius happens to express itself in unconventional fashion. People usually think that you must be either a worshipper or an opponent—perhaps in the latter case an out-and-out despiser—of a Browning, of a Walt Whitman, or in our own day of a Tolstoi. For my part I think that such writers and their works must be treated with the same freedom which they themselves exemplify. They worship nobody, and stand for themselves. Let us follow their example, so far as they themselves are concerned. In the presence of the wayward, I too may be free to judge in my own individual way. On the other hand, it is folly not to recognize how much such people and such work may mean to us, if we learn to appreciate them, not as finalities, but as individual expressions of highly significant life and thought.

II.

In the case of the *Phaenomenologie,* we must approach the work by reminding ourselves of the historical position which it occupies. The noteworthy expressions of the early idealism were formulated by a group of men most of whom were at some time at the University of Jena. Here Fichte taught between 1794 and the time when his famous controversy, due to a charge of atheism made against him, drove him from the place. Here Schelling's early works were produced. Hegel, who was five years older than Schelling and who had been a fellow-student of Schelling at Tübingen, was thirty years old in 1800. In this year he came, after a long period of preparation during which he had lived largely as a private tutor, to the University of Jena as *Privat-Docent*. He was at first understood to be a disciple of Schelling, and while he never admitted the fact, his early publications were for a time distinctly upon Schelling's side. In company with Schelling, Hegel for a time edited a philosophical journal. In 1806, the battle of Jena put a temporary stop to Hegel's opportunities at the University. In 1807, the *Phaenomenologie,* considerably delayed in publication by the troubles of the time, made its appearance. For some years thereafter Hegel was obliged to engage in other than academic occupations. Not until 1812 did he gain a place as professor of philosophy at Heidelberg, where he remained until his transfer to Berlin. The *Phaenomenologie* is, thus, subsequent to the publication of Schelling's principal useful works. It presupposes readers acquainted with the problems of recent idealism; and as already indicated, it treats even highly trained students with great severity. With very little explanation, Hegel at once introduces a distinctly new and decidedly complex philosophical vocabulary, whose meaning one is to discover mainly from the uses to which he applies it—his own deliberate opinion being that philosophical terminology can only be perfectly defined by means of considerations which can first occur to mind only at that point in the portrayal system where the vocabulary comes to be needed. Moreover, what the German historians of literature have called the barbarism of Hegel's language was due partly, as I understand, to his Suabian habits of speech, and partly to his efforts to translate all philosophical terminology that could be so treated out of Latin and Greek into a German vocabulary—an undertaking in which he showed a characteristic awkwardness. Pedagogically speaking, Hegel is distinctly austere. The learner shall adjust himself to the master. The master does comparatively little to smooth the learner's way.

The philosophical presuppositions of the book which the reader is to have in mind, he now superficially knows. The world of reality is to be defined in terms of whatever constitutes the true nature and foundation of the self. The categories of thought are to be deduced in the double sense with which we are now familiar. That is, one is to undertake what Kant attempted in his deduction of the categories, i.e., the proof that phenomena must in form be subject to the laws of thought. One must also undertake to show by a systematic development, what the forms of thought are. The book intends that the reader shall be interested in such an undertaking and shall be in general prepared to investigate the problem of life and of nature from this idealistic point of view. The method of the *Phaenomenologie* involves the demand that the reader should be pretty well acquainted with modern philosophical literature. Hegel does not cite his predecessors by name. He persistently uses the form of mere allusion; and since many of his allusions are to essays and discussions which are no longer in the forefront of our historical consciousness, we are constantly baffled in our efforts to see the force of the allusions themselves.

Meanwhile Hegel is convinced of the fundamental importance of the dialectical method. In his mind, this method has become much more systematic and elaborate than it was in the hands of Fichte, decidedly more conscious and explicit as an instrument of philosophical thought than it was for Schelling. In the *Phaenomenologie* the dialectical method appears from the start in

what I have before called its pragmatic form. The antithetical stages, the contradictory phases through which
imperfect thought passes, and inevitably passes, on its
way towards truth, are to be viewed in this book as constituting a series of stages which are represented both in
the history of science and in the history of civilization.
For philosophy the dialectical method will be the portrayal of the nature and development of the thinking
process. But this thinking process will go through a
series of phases corresponding to the successive stages
of various processes, such as occur in the lives of individuals and of nations. As these stages are represented in
personal and in social life, they will, in general, be bound
up with forms of activity and of emotion, with human
passions and conflicts. What in the logical philosophy
appears as a conflict of categories, of points of view, of
theses and antitheses, will appear in human life as a conflict of moral and of social tendencies, of opinions for
which men make sacrifices, upon which they stake their
fortunes. The conflicts of philosophical ideas will thus
appear as a kind of shadowy repetition, or representation, of the struggles of humanity for life and for light.
The thesis that history itself is a dialectical process, gets
its relative justification from that dialectical character
of the will upon which I have insisted in previous lectures. It is easy to say that in Hegel's treatment of his
ethico-logical parallelism, as one might call it, he becomes
a formalist, and often appears to falsify history by interpreting its catastrophes and its warfare in terms of
the categories of his system. But this offense, in so far
as it can be charged against Hegel, is much less present
in the *Phaenomenologie* than in his much later lectures
on the philosophy of history. For the *Phaenomenologie*

uses so much freer a method of illustrating philosophy by history, pretends so little to being a literal reproduction of past events, undertakes so obviously the task of merely expressing in its own way the spirit, the general sense, the outline of historical processes, that Hegel is here much less definitely committed than he was later to the theory that history is a literal expression in life of the categories of the philosophical logic.

On the contrary, the *Phaenomenologie* unites logic and history rather by means of a reducing of the thinking process to pragmatic terms than by means of a false translation of real life into the abstract categories of logic. It becomes manifest throughout the work that, for Hegel, thought is inseparable from will, that logic exists only as the logic of life, and the truth, although in a sense that we shall hereafter consider absolute, exists only in the form of a significant life process, in which the interests and purposes both of humanity and of the Absolute express themselves. The deduction of the categories of the thinking process, in so far as it is suggested in this work, is dialectical. It is based upon the method of antithesis, a method possessing for Hegel pragmatic significance and illustrating the way in which men live as well as the way in which men must think.

I have indicated in a most general way the philosophical interest to which the *Phaenomenologie* appeals—an interest in the new idealism, in the Kantian deduction of the categories, in the use of the dialectical method as the truly philosophical method, and in the relation of philosophy to life, of thought and will. But for this very reason Hegel conceived, as he planned this work, that an introduction to philosophy might take the form of a portrayal of a series of stages, that is, varieties of consciousness and of life, through which the mind proceeds as it passes from its natural or primal conditions towards philosophical insight. These stages Hegel is disposed to view as at once philosophically necessary and capable of historical illustration in the lives of individuals and of society. The parallelism of logic and of history, of the dialectical process and of the evolution of humanity, appears to him of service as aiding in the introduction of the learner to philosophy. That in working out the theory of this parallelism Hegel is unsuccessful, that the unprepared reader is confounded rather than led to a correct appreciation of his philosophy—this is simply Hegel's fortune as a teacher. It is his personal characteristic always to make a learner's first impression of his doctrines as puzzling as possible. He can enlighten you only after he has first, like a severe elder relative, long worried you. The actual view regarding the nature of this parellelism becomes clear only to one who knows more about the spirit of the Hegelian doctrine than the first readers of this book could have known.

Granting, however, that Hegel's system can be introduced through a study of this parallelism of logic and real life, the first problem to be solved by Hegel lay in the fact that the forms or types of consciousness which he wishes to portray appear to him to be in part stages which the moral development of an individual person will exemplify, and in part stages which the evolution of society embodies. In our sketch of Schelling we have already seen how, according to that philosopher, the stages of self-expression of the principle called the self, are partly individual, partly social, and partly impersonal. Hegel had learned from Schelling to view the expressions of the self as indeed a series of stages, logically connected, but differing in the way in which they emphasize impersonal and personal, individual and social types of consciousness. Hegel is decidedly less interested than Schelling in a philosophical comprehension of external nature, his own very vast erudition mainly related to literary, philosophical, historical, and social aspects of human life, so it is natural that his *Phaenomenologie* should be built up especially on the lines suggested by what he takes to be logically significant forms and series of personal and of social experience. It is a natural device to present the individual and the social types in two divisions, united by the fact that the individual types as such are repeated, although upon higher and more significant levels, when the individual is viewed as he ought to be, namely, in conjunction with the social order with which every phase of individual consciousness is always in fact connected.

III.

But still another and different consideration has to be mentioned in order that the structure of the *Phaenomenologie* be understood. This consideration has been singularly overlooked by most of those who have given an account of the work. Goethe's *Wilhelm Meister* had made prominent at that time a type of romance which is now no longer familiar to our readers of current literature, although it is a type which is not without its imitations in English literature. Readers of former periods were well acquainted with the form in question as it appeared in several different European literatures. What I have in mind may still better be suggested if I ask you to compare *Wilhelm Meister* with Carlyle's *Sartor*

Resartus. I refer to the romance whose hero is interesting to us principally as a type, not so much as an elementally attractive personality. It readily lent itself to the didactic purpose, and therefore from the romance of this type to the philosophical treatise there is an indefinitely graded series of intermediate forms, such as *Sartor Resartus* suggests to our minds. Such romances are prone to lay stress upon some significant process of evolution, through which the hero passes. He himself represents a type of personal experience, or development of character. The effect of such work is rather to present to us the world, or some portion of it, as seen from a typical or characteristic, and in so far personal point of view, rather than to interest us directly in the passions or in the tragedy or comedy of the hero's life. In the German literature of this period numerous instances appear, of various grades of importance. Novalis in his *Heinrich von Ofterdingen* undertook to sketch the career of a typical romantic poet, such as Novalis himself hoped to be. The romance remained unfinished. It is said to have been one of a series which Novalis planned. Each one of the series was to present a special type of personality. In the mentioned romance, as you see, the interest lies in the fact that the hero is the ideal poet, and less in the fact that he is an individual of elemental significance such as Macbeth or Romeo might possess. Art, to be sure, is always of the typical, but in work of this kind the type is chosen in cold blood, and the hero is created to fill, as it were, a somewhat abstractly defined order or demand. In art of the other sort, the hero is an individual, and becomes a type merely by virtue of the inherent and perhaps unconscious requirements of the artist's genius. Goethe's *Faust* is an individual first and a type only as a result of the greatness of the creation. But *Wilhelm Meister* is rather a typical process of natural development than primarily a personality. Ludwig Tieck had more than once used the form of the type-romance, created to present an illustration of a plan of development, or of decadence. Thus his early work, *William Lovell,* is on the whole a type-romance. Now under the influence of the literary habits of the time, it unquestionably occurred to Hegel to make his portrayal of what he calls the experience of the *Geist,* or typical mind of the race, something that could be narrated in a story, or in a connected series of stories in which typical developments are set forth. The *Phaenomenologie* therefore appears on the one hand as a sort of biography of the world-spirit—a biography in which instead of concrete events one has only the comedies and tragedies of the inner life, and these depicted rather as fortunes which occur to ideas, to purposes, if you choose, to categories, than as occurrences in the ordinary world. The name world-spirit, *Weltgeist,* which Hegel sometimes uses, and which became current in the later idealistic literature, means much the same as the term self which we have employed throughout this discussion, in a universal sense. Only the term "world-spirit" is explicitly allegorical. It refers to the self, viewed as the subject to whom historical or other human events and processes occur, so that it is as if this world-spirit lived its life by means of, or suffered and enjoyed its personal fortunes through these historical and individual processes. The world-spirit, then, is the self viewed metaphorically as the wanderer through the course of history, the incarnate god to whom the events of human life may be supposed to happen, or if you will the divinity in disguise, like Wotan the Wanderer. The term is never a technically philosophical term. But it is very frequently employed in this somewhat metaphorical sense by philosophers.

Well, the *Phaenomenologie* may be viewed, then, as the biography of the world-spirit; and somewhat in this sense Hegel conceives the plan of all except the introductory portion of his work. This life of the world-spirit consists, however, of a series of what we have called stages, and these may be compared to different incarnations or transmigrations, as it were, of the world-spirit— an interpretation which Hegel never, I think, explicitly mentions, although one passage in his preface strongly suggests the thought. The passage uses, with regard to the world-spirit, Hamlet's word addressed to his father's ghost: "What, ho, old mole, canst work in the earth so fast?" For so, says Hegel, one is sometimes tempted to say on observing through what toilsome and underground pathways of hard-won experience the spirit seems to find its way through the history of humanity to the light of reason. A frequent suggestion of this interpretation is furnished by the fact that Hegel is often describing the typical point of view which we know has received, or is receiving, its expression solely through some one person, or class of persons, whose life or lives are in the natural world wholly confined to the expression of this one phase of consciousness. Such individuals cannot rise above just that stage. Nevertheless, at the close of such a stage, Hegel speaks of "consciousness" as passing on to the next higher stage, which is such cases may be represented in the human world as we know it by wholly different individuals. The metaphor of a transmigration becomes, under these circumstances, almost inevitable as we try to follow what happens. The term used by Hegel for these various typical stages in the progress of consciousness, or of the world-spirit, is *Gestalten des Bewussteins,* that is, forms of consciousness. These forms, however, are often sharply individuated, treated as if they were persons—heroes such as are portrayed in *Wilhelm Meister* or in *Sartor Resartus.* They have their fortunes, their confident beginning, when they are sure of themselves and of their own truth, their conflicts, their enemies, their tragedy, or on occasion their comedy of contradiction, their downfall, and their final suggestion of some higher form that in a new life is to spring out of them. Side by side with this deliberate personification of an idea there runs through the text an elaborate dialectical analysis; this quasi-biography of an incarnation of the world-spirit is associated with a logical criticism of a typical opinion, or of the rationality of a certain resolution or motive or mental attitude—all this is characteristic of the baffling, but deliberate, method of the work. The presentation is very generally saved from mere pedantry, such as an elaborate logical analysis of what is all the time viewed as a live creature, might readily entail. It is saved by the novelty of the mode of treatment, by the remarkable union of a sensitive appreciation with a merciless critical analysis; in brief, by the author's genius and by his genuine philosophical interest.

The usual character of the biography of any one of these *Gestalten* is as follows. Each expresses an attitude, an idea, and so a mode of behavior, a reaction towards the world, which at each stage appears inevitably to grow out of previous stages. Any such stage of consciousness presents itself, therefore, as inevitable, as rational, as the only way to live and to think, as *the* interpretation, of life, of thought, and of the universe. As a fact, so Hegel frequently assures us, each of these forms expresses in its own way, and according to its own lights, the genuine nature of the self. Within its own limits, each of these forms *is* the truth. It possesses in general "the certainty that it is all reality." As a fact, however, it implies some sort of contrast between a subjective and an objective aspect, present either within what it regards as itself, or in its relation to what it regards as its external world. In other words, each of these forms exemplifies some aspect of the problem of self-consciousness, some aspect of the problem as to the relation between thought and reality. And this problem also appears in every such case as having more or less of practical, of passionate, or at least of significant and interesting value. The theoretical problems always appear as also life problems. The *Gestalt* in question, the *Weltgeist* thus incarnate, first becomes aware of its problem by noting that it has not yet fully and consciously expressed, and found, what it means. Is it a contemplative observer of facts? Then it has not yet seen just how these facts are related to its own nature. Is it rather a practical attitude towards the world, an attitude of ambition, of protest, of rebellion, of reform? Then it has not yet carried out its work. It must proceed to fight its battle and to express itself. As the *Gestalt* thus undertakes the work of its little life, or on higher stages, of its worldwide expression, it at once must develop what is within and come in conflict with what is without. The result is, often enough, so far as this *Gestalt* is concerned, either comic or tragic in the resulting dialectic. The calm confidence of its beginning, or, so to speak, of its youth, turns as it proceeds into disappointment, into contradiction, into a more or less logical repentance. Its ideas prove to be fantastic, its supposed facts turn out to be dreams; its sincerity is exposed through the experience of life and through a merciless self-criticism, and then proves to be, sometimes self-deception, sometimes hypocrisy, frequently both. The destiny of its life is determined on the whole by a formula characteristic of Hegel's view of the dialectic method. Its external conflicts with the world that it views as its object or as other than itself, turn out to be also essentially internal conflicts. That is, for its own difficulties, it blames the world at first, but discovers that the fault is its own. On the other hand, its internal diremption, its inner contradiction, always expresses itself in external conflicts. And just this unity of the external and internal is what furnishes the positive result of the process which upon each stage is carried out. What the *Gestalt* has falsely regarded as its own, proves to be due to what it had thought to be the utterly foreign world. On the other hand, whatever it finds in its world proves to be in turn the development, or the expression, of its own nature. Hence its failure implies a reconstruction of the view regarding itself and its world, with which it had begun. What it had called its own comes to seem foreign to it. What it had called utterly remote, and merely a not-self, turns out to be its own flesh and blood. In its own special form, then, this typical incarnation of the world-spirit passes away. But it gives place to an enriched view of the nature of things, which takes form in some new type of consciousness.

As the reader follows this series of typical forms of consciousness, he is constantly impressed with the mercilessly negative criticism which at every stage greets whatever at the outset seems most individual of each *Gestalt*, and most sacred from its point of view. That in developing such an attitude Hegel is constantly inspired by a sense of the stern judgment that life and history in his day had passed upon human illusion and upon false efforts, is obvious enough. But the criticism in question is characteristic of the philosopher's own technical method. As dialectician, as exposer of contradictions, as negative adept in reflection, Hegel has learned from Socrates, from the Platonic dialogues, from the Kantian antinomies, from Fichte, and from Schelling's joyous fondness for paradoxes. The negative procedure on its technical side, is deliberate, minute, and often wearisome. It is represented at each stage by the philosopher not as his own external comment but as the internal development and experience of the *Gestalt* in question. But the reader learns to feel a sympathy for each successive incarnation of the *Weltgeist*, as conscious in the beginning of its own universal and divine mission, it sets out upon its career of world conquest, arrayed with all the spoils that have been accumulated by the labors of its predecessors, only to find itself ere long fast bound in the net of its own contradictions, and ending its days like a blinded Samson, a victim to the Philistines who are, after all, in this idealistic world, only its own thoughts. As a fact, Hegel regards and expressly proclaims the principle of what he here calls ''negativity'' as the principle both of the world process and of philosophical logic. Thus the dialectical method reaches in this work an explicitness not previously known in philosophical literature. But it must not be supposed that Hegel himself viewed this process as purely negative. In his introduction to the work, and repeatedly in the course of his discussion, he points out that each of these negative discoveries, however tragic from the point of view of the life, that is, of the idea or opinion or attitude concerned, is in fact also a positive discovery, a new revelation as to the inter-relation of the mind and of things, a new proof that in the realm of experience subject and object are not to be sundered, and that their unity develops out of the very conflicts which appear to exist between them so long as their relations are imperfectly appreciated.

Rosenkranz in his biography of Hegel, narrates an oft-cited story of how in later years, when Hegel was at Heidelberg, a company of students to whom he was one evening in private conversation expounding some aspects and results of the dialectic method, listened with a certain terror to the apparently destructive attack upon various traditional views; so that when Hegel at length rose and left, one of the students exclaimed, as he watched the retreating figure, "That is nobody but death himself, and so must everything pass away." (*Das sei der Tod selber, und so müsse alles vergehen.*) Another who was present had caught the positive undertone and outcome of the discussion, and expressed himself more cheerfully. As a fact, it was Hegel's characteristic view that all such negations mean, when viewed as it were from above, the inner self-differentiation of the life of the spirit, the enrichment of its existence through manifold finite expressions, which in their very variety and mutual opposition supplement one another, and together express the totality of a true life. The truth, says Hegel, in the introduction to the *Phaenomenologie*, "is the whole." And because the truth is the whole, the utmost power of negation is powerless to prevent the world-spirit from coming to life in new forms, or from expressing, through the higher wealth which these new forms contain, the positive results, which, for Hegel, are the inevitable outcome of the lower stages.

IV.

We are now prepared to sketch a little more connectedly the way in which the *Phaenomenologie* is built up. In the course of the preface which has become famous as the first formal statement of the programme of the coming Hegelian system of philosophy, Hegel announces that instead of beginning his proposed system with a direct account of the proof, he undertakes to prepare the way for philosophy by recounting the experience through which consciousness passes from naïve to philosophical insight. The plan of defining a series of *Gestalten* is outlined. The relation of the logical examination of these stages to their character as forms present in the course of the life-history of humanity, is set forth. By the word "consciousness" Hegel means a mental process, in so far as it stands over against and opposed to some sort of fact or object. He defines in general the problem of consciousness as the problem of determining its own relation to its object. This relation cannot be determined without passing through a succession of views in which both the consciousness in question and the object of this consciousness are altered through reflection and through an experience of the problems of the situation. Consciousness, as he indicates in beginning the enterprise, will appear upon four distinct stages. First it appears as mere consciousness, that is, as the knowing process which finds a world of facts over against it, and which simply examines these facts to find what is certain or true about them. The second is the stage of self-consciousness, that is, of the essentially idealistic view, which regards its object as in somewise the expression of itself. The third is the stage of reason, in which the objects of consciousness exist as the relatively impersonal embodiment of ideas, but in such wise that this highly categorized world, is regarded by the self as still identical in principle with its own constitution, so that the attitude of consciousness is expressible thus: There is indeed a world, and a real one, but this world is essentially mine, to comprehend by my science, or to conquer by my will, in short, to possess, not as my private caprice, but as my universally valid truth. The fourth stage of consciousness is called *Geist,* that is, mind or spirit, in its fully concrete or explicit sense. The world of the spirit is the world which consists not only of my universally valid truth, but of my conscious truth, as is expressed by a social order to which I belong, by a humanity in whose life I take part. At the summit of the world of the spirit, as its absolute expression, appears a form or series of forms of consciousness, which in the table of contents of the *Phaenomenologie* is formally sundered from the *Geist* proper, that is, from the social type of consciousness. This is the consciousness of what one might call the super-social or religious realm, the last realm where consciousness pauses before it becomes explicitly and reflectively philosophical.

In treating the first of these forms, namely *Bewusstein,* or simple consciousness, Hegel makes no attempt at introducing the quasi-biographical form which we have discussed in the foregoing. This, which is the introductory discussion of the text, contains an elaborate dialectical proof of the general thesis of idealism. The ground covered is somewhat similar to that which one finds covered in Fichte and in Schelling, although the argument is decidedly novel. The text is here, especially at a first reading, extremely difficult, and has unquestionably served to render the book esoteric, from the point of view of most readers. What is characteristic of the *Phaenomenologie* begins with the second stage, with self-consciousness. Hegel's treatment is here founded upon the thought that, although a technical idealism is confined to the philosophers, every human being is practically, that is, in what we might now call the pragmatic sense, an idealist. For it is of the nature of a rational being to assert himself as the central reality of the world, and then to attempt to interpret all that he finds in terms of his own interests. So herewith the union of logical analysis with typical portrayal of human character and destiny begins. The first stage of self-consciousness is represented by the naïve individualism of the child or of the savage. The movement present upon this stage is determined by the fact upon which Fichte and Schelling had insisted, by the fact that the self in order to be individual, must needs be, however crudely, social, that is, must know itself by contrast with the other. Hence the first expression of self-consciousness in the form of crude individualism, observes itself by virtue of contrast with the other self who appears as the intruder and disturber, that is, as false self in the world of the savage individual. "I am the self; but who are you?" Such is the attitude in terms of which the savage, or the boy, greets the stranger. Hence the natural condition of the crude self is indeed one of warfare with its kind. This primitive stage, essentially self-destructive, quickly gives place to stages of self-consciousness which involve still crude but intense forms of higher individualism. As the self grows, its world becomes more complex; and at the stage of rea-

158

son we pass to forms of consciousness which are still
individual, but which appear with a highly rational or
elaborately categorized world over against them, in which
they seek their victory or their task, in terms which are
not only individualistic, but also explicitly universal, so
that each *Gestalt* seeks what it views as that which all the
world is seeking. The world of *Geist* next appears as a
series of incarnations of the self, which are no longer
individual, but explicitly universal, and also social. In
other words, these *Gestalten* are now entire societies, nations, stages of culture, or on higher levels, movements
of thought and of general social action,—reforms, recon-
stitutions of society, institutions possessing spiritual
significance.

The chronological relations which these various forms
are conceived to have, involves a complication only gradually explained in the text; the *Gestalten* of self-consciousness and of reason are contemporaneous with those
of the *Geist*. That is, there are certain forms of individuality, which are found in, and are characteristic of,
certain social types; and which therefore in time appear
along with the latter. But for the sake of the dialectical
analysis, the forms of self-consciousness and of reason
are analyzed before the forms of the *Geist*. A similar link
connects certain forms of the religious consciousness with
certain stages in the history of the *Geist*. Yet the forms
of the religious consciousness are never treated in their
entirety until after the forms of the social mind have
been successively presented.

So much for a first sketch of the plan of the *Phaenomenologie*. Its outcome, viewed as a dialectical achieve-
ment, is to be the definition of a form of consciousness
which is to be identical with the philosophical conscious-

ness itself. Philosophy appears, in Hegel's account, as the result of the lesson of the world's history. Yet this result does not depend merely upon transcending, but upon including all the forms of experience and of self-expression which have been learned by the way. The philosophical definition of the nature of the self, and of its relation to the world, will be possible only upon the basis of an appreciation of the forms under which the self expresses itself in the history of humanity. The lesson of history will be transformed by philosophy into the law of logic. Yet on the other hand, the logical development is dependent upon, and in its own abstract way will repeat, the development that the mind gets, through practical conflict with the world and with itself. The history of the human will, and of its purification through conflict and through tragedy, will be reflected in the realm of pure thought in the sequence of categories, and in the definition of truth.

Fichte, as you remember, had defined an ethical idealism. Schelling had added an effort to unify idealism and natural history, and had found the culmination of his doctrine at the moment when he wrote the work which we at the last time reviewed, in a philosophy of art. Hegel begins by conceiving that the logic of history, or more generally, the logic of human activity and of the human will, is a natural preliminary to the comprehension of theoretical truth.

LECTURE VII.

TYPES OF INDIVIDUAL AND SOCIAL CONSCIOUSNESS IN HEGEL'S *PHAENOMENOLOGIE*.

IN beginning the present discussion, it seems worth while to state a little more explicitly than was done at the last time how the argument of the *Phaenomenologie des Geistes* is related to the general problem of idealism, i.e., the problem of defining the relation between the external, or apparently external, world of experience and the nature of the self.

I.

The interest of Hegel, as of all the idealists, is in defining, so far as possible, the true nature of this relation. Yet in the *Phaenomenologie,* which is an introduction to a philosophy and not a system of philosophy itself, such a deduction of the true relations of the self and the world cannot be completely stated. People often suppose that such a work as the *Phaenomenologie* is an effort to deduce a priori both the forms and the contents which the various stages of consciousness must necessarily assume. The reader who comes to the work in this spirit inevitably asks, when Hegel mentions a given form of individual, of social, or of religious consciousness, "Why must just this form of consciousness exist at all? How do you know that such a form exists? Do you know it otherwise than by your ordinary experience as a plain man? If so, do you not pretend to deduce what you actually find as a fact of human nature?" In answer to this objection, it may be said that Hegel repeatedly and plainly admits that in the course of the *Phaenomenologie* he is not "deducing" the existence of the various forms of consciousness mentioned in so far as they belong to our concrete experience of human life. He is merely using them as illustrations of the stages which are indeed demanded by the logic of the process of evolution of consciousness. At a given stage a problem appears. It is developed. Its difficulties are made manifest. In so far the student of the problem becomes aware of a certain logical differentiation which the various phases or aspects of the problem have assumed in his own mind. Under these circumstances he turns to life and finds there a form of practical, of common-sense, of personal, or of social activity which expresses in its own way substantially the same problem as the one with which he is dealing. In the *Phaenomenologie* Hegel hereupon uses the known characteristics and fortunes of this type of human life or of human consciousness as an illustration of the present phase of his problem. In this way one can understand a little better what at first sight seems very mysterious, namely the relation of Hegel's discussion to the chronological sequence of the stages he is analyzing. At certain points in his discussion it appears as if he regarded the chronological sequence of the stages of civilization as correspondent to the logical sequence of the stages of the problem that he is defining. And to some extent this is indeed the case. On the other hand, there are cases where the chronological sequence of the stages of consciousness in question is either, to our minds, entirely indeterminate

or decidedly distinct from the logical sequence of the
phases of the philosophical problem which Hegel is en-
gaged in developing. Thus in the early part of that section of the *Phaenomenologie,* entitled *Geist,* where stages
of civilization are especially in question, Hegel seems to
be dealing first with relatively primitive, and then with
relatively much more highly developed types of civilization. One is tempted, in view of the illustrations used, to
suppose for a while that the chronology of European history is in question. It seems in consequence purely
fantastic when, in characterizing the mental life of what
one might call the imperial type, Hegel makes a rapid
and unexplained transition from his characterization of
Roman civilization, to the characterization of the French
monarchy of Louis XIV. The uninitiated reader asks at
once, ''What has become of the Middle Ages?'' Again, in
the earlier portions of the *Phaenomenologie* where Hegel
is treating rather types of individuals than types of society, a series of phases of consciousness appears, containing, for instance, the consciousness of a savage at war
with his fellow men; the consciousness of the stoic independent of all fortunes; the consciousness of the religious
devotee, shut up in his cell and longing for a mystical
union with a wholly indefinite and perfect deity; the
consciousness of a Faust, as the early Faust fragment
of Goethe defined that consciousness; the consciousness
of a knight-errant, a sort of Don Quixote seeking in ad-
venturous contest with the world his self-possession; the
consciousness of a group of pedantic scholars criticizing
one another's productions—in brief, we find a series of
forms of personality which seems to be the result of a decidedly arbitrary, although interesting, selection. One
asks at once as to the chronological relations of these

forms of personality. One feels that they do not belong to any one determinate temporal sequence. Yet the correspondence between the evolution of humanity and the logical evolution of a problem seems to be more or less a guiding principle with Hegel. The result, however, is baffling.

All these varieties of expression are to be understood in the light of the consideration just mentioned. The *Phaenomenologie* is not responsible for the philosophy of history. It *is* responsible for the use of historical types as illustration of stages of the evolution of a rational consciousness. It finds the illustrations empirically. It analyzes them logically. It is led by the analysis from stage to stage.

But there are cases where the chronological relation itself becomes important; in such instances Hegel himself is likely to inform us explicitly that this is so. There are connected historical processes whose connection Hegel views as mainly a logical one. Such instances Hegel finds in the inevitable decay of small states, a decay which he believes to be due to the inner logical instability of their distinctly local or essentially provincial ideals. A world of small communities must give place, for reasons which Hegel regards as logical, to a world of an imperial type of social unity. And yet, Hegel himself views the process whereby this is accomplished as a process involving wars whose outcome he declares to be accidental—that is, these wars, whereby the imperial unity is indeed attained, are not determined in their details by the logical process in question. Another instance, very important for the general structure of the *Phaenomenologie,* is furnished by the dissolution of the imperial type of society through the attainment of individual independence on the part of the citizens, and a consequent rebellion against authority, whose direct result tends to be anarchy. Hegel, writing as he does in a period immediately subsequent to the French Revolution and at a time when the future constitution of Europe was entirely doubtful, speaks of this process not as one that constitutes the ultimate goal of human civilization but as one which to his mind is presumably destined to occur in a rhythmic way again and again in the course of human history. Thus provincialism leads to imperialism, imperialism to culture, and culture to a highly sophisticated individualism. Individualism, let loose, leads then to a temporary anarchy. And so, as Hegel in this book views the philosophy of social processes, the social mind returns, through the condition of anarchy which is a sort of temporary relapse into savagery to the beginning of its life, and repeats, possibly in an almost circular way, the stages of its merely political self-expression. The logical lesson seems, so far, to be that, as Hegel conceived the matter in the early years of the nineteenth century, genuine stability, rational unity of consciousness, cannot be achieved upon a purely social basis. The logical outcome of the failure of man to give to the social order a permanent structure in the visible world is, in the *Phaenomenologie,* the transition to the religious, and through the religious, to the philosophical consciousness.

The evolution of religion itself Hegel defines in the closing section of the book as somewhat parallel to the social evolution. Only the chronological evolution of religion is of another type. As a higher manifestation of the *Geist,* religion develops not in a circle, with a return to essentially the same anarchy as that with which it begins, but rather in a straight line, from a vague recognition of the divine in the powers of nature to the entire identification of the divine principle with the principle of a rational self-consciousness. The stages of the religious consciousness are at once logical and chronological, although it must here also be said that, in his sketch, Hegel considers only what he regards as the essential forms of religion, and does not attempt to predetermine such processes as are exemplified by the long struggle amongst various religions, as for instance by the struggle between Mohammedanism and Christianity. Such matters he entirely ignores in his account of the development of the religious consciousness. They belong to those aspects of the historical life which a complete philosophy of history might have to consider, but which the *Phaenomenologie,* which is merely seeking illustrations, may wholly ignore.

When we remember that the entire series of those forms of personal and social life which are depicted in the *Phaenomenologie,* is preceded, in the first part of the book, by an exposition of a series of views of the nature of things which is distinctly a series of philosophical theories or conceptions, and is not a series of phases, either of the consciousness of persons or of the social consciousness, we see to how limited a degree the structure of the *Phaenomenologie* is dependent upon the thesis that psychology and the history of sociology can at once be interpreted in purely logical terms.

II.

Before we go further, it is worth while to dwell upon a brief sketch of the relation of the *Phaenomenologie* to the purely philosophical outcome which Hegel is seeking. This outcome, as we know, is to be an absolute idealism. The thesis to be obtained is that all being, all life, all nature, all personal and all social consciousness, are expressions of the meaning of a single Absolute, whose experience is determined by one universal or necessary ideal. This Absolute is that which is directly expressed in self-consciousness, in so far as self-consciousness is rational. In contrast with Schelling, Hegel lays much less stress upon the physical order of external things, and upon the unconscious aspect of mental life. He constantly recognizes the unconscious; but for him unconsciousness exists, so to speak, as an aspect of a given and concrete conscious process, as when a man who is busy with practical life is unconscious of the motives that lie at the basis of his practical activities, or as when a man who is busy in a reasoning process is unconscious of the formal logic of that process. It is the destiny of Hegel's Absolute to be expressed in conscious form. Hegel insists that this conscious form must always be an individual form. The Absolute must come to consciousness as an individual, or as a system of conscious individuals. With respect to the question as to whether the Absolute in its wholeness is a conscious being, the *Phaenomenologie* is distinctly ambiguous in its result. In the closing chapter of the book, where the results are outlined, it at once appears that the Absolute is a consciousness of the meaning of the entire human process, and that for the absolute consciousness, the various *Gestalten*, the various phases of life, are in a genuine meaning present, and present at once. But since in this closing chapter Hegel is especially describing the philosophical type of consciousness itself, there is at least a strong indication that the consciousness which he here attributes to the Absolute is identical merely with the consciousness expressed in philosophy. The prevailing indication of the text would be that the Absolute comes to its com· pletest form of consciousness in rational individuals who, as seers or as thinkers, become aware of the rational na- ture of the entire process of rational life. I do not myself believe that this view of the matter remained for Hegel final. I believe that the sense of his later religious philosophy, as stated in his mature system, demands the reality of a conscious Absolute, whose consciousness, while inclusive of that of the rational human individuals and in fact of all finite beings, is not identical with the mere sum-total of these individual consciousnesses. But it is true that this result is not made manifest in the *Phaenomenologie*. It is also true that Hegel always expressed himself so ambiguously upon the subject that a well-known difference of opinion as to his true meaning appeared amongst his followers. This difference led to the division and ultimately to the dissolution of the Hegelian school.

Without attempting to consider whether the form in which the final or absolute consciousness gets embodied— that is, without attempting to decide whether it is God apart from the philosopher, who timelessly knows the meaning of the entire process of the finite world, or whether the divine consciousness appears only as the philosophical consciousness—we may, in any case, characterize the general nature of this absolute consciousness, or as Hegel calls it at the end of the *Phaenomenologie*, the *absolutes Wissen* as follows: The Absolute whose expression is the world and, in particular, the world of human life, is a being characterized by a complete unity or harmony of what one might call a theoretical and practical consciousness. The theoretical consciousness is a consciousness which views facts and endeavors to apprehend them. The practical consciousness is a consciousness which constructs facts in accordance with its ideals. The absolute consciousness is both theoretical and practical. Furthermore, the abolute consciousness is a self-consciousness, in the sense which Schelling had already tried to define; it contains nothing which is not its own object. It is nothing which is not known to itself. It is, therefore, a complete and organic union of a subjective and of an objective aspect. Meanwhile, as we now know, the Hegelian thesis as to the structure of this Absolute Being involves the recognition that the dialectical method tells us an essential, or one might perhaps say *the* essential, truth with regard to the life of the Absolute. The true rational self-consciousness cannot express itself except in the form of a series of incomplete manifestations, which the complete consciousness interrelates, reconciles through a view of their interrelations, but at the same time demands as its own necessary expression. In other words, an Absolute which is not expressed in finite form is impossible.

On the other hand, a finite expression of consciousness which is not defective, self-conflicting, and in its finitude self-defeating, is impossible. The only way in which the perfect can express itself is through the imperfect. The Absolute cannot know itself except in terms of a finite world. Every stage and phase of this finite world must be defective, incomplete, self-contradictory, and when temporally viewed, transient, precisely in so far as it is finite. To be sure, throughout the entire process of finite defeat and decay, categories, types, structures, and what the ordinary consciousness calls substances, the natures of things may and do persist. But the life of the world is not in this, its permanent structure. For this permanent structure is only the abstract aspect of things. The life of the world has to be expressed in a series of forms, each of which is transient, while the relation between them is the dialectical relation. That is, each lower form, contradicting itself, and in so far passing away, finds what Hegel calls its truth upon a higher stage. Yet the lower form in turn can insist that without it the higher stage would be logically impossible. Indeed the lower form in some sense persists, preserves its meaning, as an organic part of the higher form. The immortal soul of whatever has decayed is temporarily preserved in whatever succeeds it. Nothing passes away without leaving its mark. Thus the lower forms are preserved in the higher, and at the same time keep their place in the universe as a whole in a two-fold way.

This is the two-fold way. The true view of life, of consciousness, of history, of the universe, is essentially a non-temporal point of view, which sees at once all these phases as, each in its place, necessary. But in so far as the phases are viewed as sequent one to another in time, the later phases include the immortal meaning of the earlier phases. In expressing this last doctrine Hegel lays considerable stress upon a thesis which has become well-known in connection with the later doctrine of evolution. Every individual recapitulates in his development the phases of individual life which have temporally preceded him; so that every individual in his evolution is a mirror of the entire process of temporal evolution, up to the stage which he himself occupies. Hegel's theory of the Absolute is therefore at once, and in a way which is not very clearly explained, an evolutionary theory *and* a non-temporal theory. The absolute consciousness is an inclusion in a single non-temporal consciousness of the meaning of all temporal processes. But, on the other hand, the absolute consciousness is the goal of an historical process. Viewed in its latter aspect the evolutionary relation of the absolute consciousness seems peculiarly puzzling, for one inevitably asks Hegel, what is it that is to happen next, now that by hypothesis in some form the absolute consciousness has been attained by the discovery of the meaning of the whole history? But such questions go beyond what it is now necessary to consider in our attempt to grasp the general significance of this idealistic doctrine.

III.

If we turn to the study of the special phases through which consciousness passes, as these are depicted in the *Phänomenologie,* we find that the defects of the imperfect phases are such as, according to the doctrine, tend of themselves to make clear the structure of the absolute consciousness. For as you have just heard, the imperfections of the finite are all of them aspects of the complete expression of the infinite or perfect self or Absolute. Let us enumerate, then, some of these defects as they come out in the course of the book. The lower stages of consciousness, whether individual or social, may first be viewed as divided into two types. They are stages where the finite subject, or knower of the process in question, is either too exclusively theoretical or too exclusively practical in his attitude towards his life and towards his world. The Absolute alone combines in one both of these aspects. In finite life the too exclusively practical stages may be described as in general "blind." Those who are confined to these stages are active, earnest, enthusiastic, fanatical, hopeful or heroic. But they do not rightfully grasp what it is they are trying to do. The too exclusively theoretical stages of consciousness may be described as relatively "empty." One looks on the world, but finds in it little of significance, of the ideal, of the valuable. One becomes skeptical. One mercilessly exposes the contradictions of his own abstract conceptions. One thinks; but one has so far not learned to live.

From another point of view the lower stages are distinct from the absolute consciousness. The finite self finds its world, whether this be theoretical or practical, as if it were something foreign. It fails to recognize its own unity with its world. Viewed theoretically, its facts then appear accidental or unexplained, or as if due to mysterious power. Viewed practically, the world seems to the mind uncanny or hostile. The finite self is not at home. It becomes a wanderer. It sees its destiny elsewhere. Perhaps it is in the desert, guided only by the pillar of cloud by day and by fire by night. Perhaps it is amongst its foes who must be defeated. Perhaps, like Kant, it is dealing with the mysterious thing in itself. However the foreign world appears, the defect is that the self here does not recognize this world as its own. Or again, although on higher stages it may be thoroughly sure, as heroic and confident reformers are sure, that its world is its own and truly belongs to it, or as Hegel expresses it, as *an sich*, the self, the subject, does not yet see how this is true. Obviously the defective stages may here be, as we have said, either theoretical or practical. They may also be either individual or social. Israel in the wilderness, which Hegel himself does not mention as an illustration, would stand for a society whose world is foreign and whose laws are, consequently, supposed to be merely an ideal legislation for a future commonwealth.

But the imperfect life of the finite self may be characterized in still another way. In general the finite stages of consciousness are those in which the subject assumes some special form—is, as Hegel often says, *bestimmt,* that is determined to a particular way of living or of thinking. Dialectical considerations, then, always insure that over against this special form of self-consciousness, and in so far contemporaneous with it, there must be other opposed forms of subjectivity. These opposed forms of subjectivity are, then, to any one of the determinate subjects, his enemies. And so the world assumes the type which we characterized a moment ago. From this point of view finite life appears not merely as a passing away of each stage but as a conflict upon each stage with its own enemies, who are after all identical in nature with itself.

The imperfect stages of finite consciousness may be also viewed thus: The self, anticipating its own absolute calling and destiny, confident that it does know the world, may try to express the still unclear consciousness of its absoluteness either by affirming itself as this ego, this person, or on the other hand, by sacrificing all its personality and surrendering itself to a vague Absolute. In other words, the self may be thus a conscious individualist, or a self-abnegating mystic. In its social forms, this opposition between two imperfect types of self-consciousness would be expressed, for instance, in anarchy on the one hand and despotism on the other. That is, the theory of society might be founded on the maxim, Everyone for himself; or it might be founded on the maxim, All are subject to one. Whether individual or social, this type of finite imperfection is found exemplified all the way through the series of stages.

If one contrast with these types of imperfection the type of an absolute consciousness, of the consciousness that views itself, and rightly views itself, as world-possessor and as self-possessor, this fulfilled self of the absolute knowledge must, according to Hegel, possess the following characteristics:

(1) It must be an union of theoretical and practical consciousness. It must see only what is its own deed, and must do nothing except what it understands. Precisely this, according to Hegel, is what occurs, to be sure in a highly abstract form, in the philosophical theory of the categories such as he afterwards embodied in his logic. For the categories of the Hegelian logic are at once pure thoughts and pure deeds.

(2) The absolute consciousness must be that of a self which is conscious of objects without going beyond its consciousness to find them. Such a consciousness, Hegel views as in the abstract realizable in a philosophical system.

(3) Somewhat more important still is the consideration that the Absolute must be a self that by virtue of its inmost principle appears to itself as an interrelated unity of selves without being the less one self. From this point of view Hegel calls the Absolute, *Geist*. Spirit in its complete sense is a consciousness, for which the individual exists only in social manifestation and expression, so that an individual apart from other individuals is meaningless, and so that the relations of individuals have been so completely expressed that each finds his being in all the others and exists in perfect unity with them. In his later system of philosophy this view of the nature of

spirit lies at the foundation of Hegel's interpretation of the positive theory both of society and of religion. In the *Phaenomenologie,* the highest form of spirit which appears concretely expressed in the life of humanity is the form assumed by the church, in so far as the church is in possession of a perfectly rational religion. The Holy Spirit, identical with and present in the true life of the church, is for Hegel, in the *Phaenomenologie,* the living witness to this essentially social character of the absolute consciousness. That there appears considerable doubt whether the church as Hegel conceives it in this book is precisely identical with any one of the forms which the Christian church has assumed, is a consideration which does not here further concern us.

(4) Possibly the most notable feature of the absolute consciousness is that which unites completely finite and infinite. It saves its absoluteness by assuming special embodiments. Hegel always laid very great stress upon this thesis. It is a failure to grasp it which has so often made the religious conception of the deity what Hegel regards as abstract and relatively fruitless. To conceive' God as first perfect by Himself and then, so to speak, capriciously creating a world of imperfection, this is not to conceive the divine consciousness as it is; it is perfect through the infinite imperfections of its finite expressions, and through the fact that these imperfections are nevertheless unified in its complete life. In the *Phae-. nomenologie,* this view is repeatedly insisted upon, and is expressed in connection with that phase of consciousness which Hegel calls the forgiveness of sin.

The thesis, then, in terms of which Hegel defines his Absolute is that the absolute self is aware of itself as a process involving an inner differentiation into many centers of selfhood. Each one of these centers of selfhood is, when viewed as a particular center and taken in its finitude, theoretically self-contradictory, practically evil. On the other hand, each of these finite expressions of the self is theoretically true, in so far as it represents the Universal and is related thereto; and it is practically justified, in so far as it aims at the Universal in deed and in spirit. In the religious consciousness of the forgiveness of sin, the Absolute, both as forgiving infinite and as forgiven finite, reaches this consciousness in a form which expresses the absolute process. The absolute process is, however, further expressible, apart from such images and allegories. To Hegel's mind it is inseparably associated with religion in the form of a philosophical or scientific consciousness. This philosophical consciousness explains, justifies, makes clear the existence of finitude, actuality, imperfection, sin. In the form of the dialectical method, philosophy emphasizes that contradictory and imperfect expression is necessary to the life of the infinite. In assigning to each special category its place, exhibiting its defect, and justifying this defect by its place in the whole system, philosophy expresses in the form of a rational consciousness what the religious consciousness discovers in the form of the union of the finite and infinite through the forgiveness of sin.

IV.

I turn from this indication of a very remarkable attempt to solve the problems of that time and of this type of philosophy, to a mention of some of the special illustrations. Let us confine ourselves for the moment to illustration of individual rather than of social types of consciousness. The first *Gestalt* of individual consciousness which Hegel considers is, as we said at the last time, the savage consciousness of the warrior, practically viewing himself as the only real self in the world, boasting his prowess as such, and consequently seeking to destroy whatever pretentious fellow may attempt falsely to be the self. It is because of the assurance, dim of course and purely practical, on the part of each man that he is the Absolute—it is because of this that the universal war of all against all appears. This primitive state of universal war, a conception which Hegel in so far accepts from the seventeenth-century theories of human nature, is to his mind a phase of human nature as transient as it is irrational. The reason for this transiency lies in the fact that killing a man proves nothing, except that the victor, in order to prove himself to be the self, needs still another man to kill, and is therefore essentially a social being. Even head hunting implies dependence upon one's neighbor who is good enough to furnish one more head for the hunter. Let one note this element of mutuality, and mere destruction gives way to a higher form of social consciousness. This higher stage of individual self-realization is reached in the still primitive type of society which is represented by the master and his slave. The master essentially recognizes that he needs somebody else in order that this other may prove him, the master, to be the self. The best proof that I am the self, so the master thinks, is given when another is subject to my will. Because he is another, and in so far a self, he by contrast assures me of my own selfhood; for with Hegel as with Schelling individual self-consciousness is a social contrast effect. For after all, I can only know myself as this individual if I find somebody else in the world, by contrast with whom I recognize who I am. But the master essentially hopes to prove himself to be the true self, by making the slave his mere organ, the mirror of his own functions, his will objectified. The world of the master and slave is therefore explicitly two-fold, and is not like the world of the head-hunting warriors, the world in which each man lived only by denying that the other had any right to live. The slave, to be sure, has no rights, but he has his uses, and he teaches me, the master, that I am the self. Unfortunately, however, for the master, the master hereby becomes dependent upon the slave's work. The master after all is merely the onlooker and is self only so far as he sees the other at work for him. The master's life is therefore essentially lazy and empty. Of the two, the faithful slave after all comes much nearer to genuine selfhood. For self-consciousness is practical, is active, and depends upon getting control of experience. The slave, so Hegel says, works over, reconstructs the things of experience. Therefore by his work he, after all, is conquering the world of experience, is making it the world of the self, is becoming the self. The slave is potentially, or in embryo—is *an sich,* as Hegel would say—the self-respecting man, who in the end must become justly proud of the true mastery that his work gives him. Let this essential character of the slave,—the fact that he, as worker, is the only true man in this primitive society—let this fact come to his own consciousness, and the self becomes transformed from slavery to a higher phase of consciousness. This new phase is represented in Hegel's account, curiously enough, by a form which in history appears as a stage of philosophical consciousness, namely, by stoicism.

Stoicism, however, is here viewed in its practical, and not in its theoretical, aspects as a doctrine of the world.

INDIVIDUAL AND SOCIAL CONSCIOUSNESS

Practically stoicism is the attitude of the man who regards all things with which he deals as necessarily subject to his own reason, whether he can control them physically or not; because he has found that the self, through its own rational ideal, needs no slaves, no conquest at war, to prove its independence. He is still a member of a society, but it is now an ideal society, composed of the stoic and of his ideal Reason, his guide. Through the discipline of life the stoic has become entirely indifferent to whether he is master or slave. Whether on the throne or in chains or in service, the self, and just the individual self, is self-possessed if it ideally declares itself so to be. Its social relation, its relation to another, is now simply its relation to its own ideal. I and my reason constitute the world. The dialectical defect of the stoic's position is that the actual world of the stoic's life—the world of activity, of desire, of interest—is meanwhile going on in its own accidental way. The self in order to attain independence has resigned all definite plans of control over fortunes. Its concrete life is therefore empty. If it hereupon becomes aware of this fact it turns from the stoic into the skeptic, and learns to doubt even its own present ideal. Hegel here has in mind the practical aspect of the forms of older ancient skepticism, which undertook to retain the term of rational self-consciousness by a reflection upon the vanity of all special doctrines, ideals, dogmas, assurances, concerning common life. The skeptic, a Diogenes in a tub, proves his independence by destroying convictions, by being entirely indifferent to conventions, by being essentially restless, and merely dialectical. The result of a thoroughgoing adoption of this point of view is that life gets the sort of vanity which has been well suggested to our own generation by Fitzgerald's wonderful paraphrase of the Omar Khayyam stanzas. The self is now indeed free, but life is vain; and the world has once more fallen, seemingly in a hopeless way, into chaos. The *Weltgeist*, recognizing its failure so far to win its own, must once more transmigrate.

V.

Hereupon Hegel introduces as the next *Gestalt* of individual consciousness a very remarkable one entitled, ''The Unhappy Consciousness.'' That the consciousness of the Omar Khayyam stanzas is unhappy we shall all remember. And that this unhappiness results from skepticism concerning the worth of every concrete human life, is also obvious. What Hegel notes is the substantial identity between a consciousness which is unhappy for this reason, and the consciousness which, like that expressed in well-known devotional books, such as *The Imitation of Christ,* or in the practical life of solitary religious devotees of all faiths, views its unhappiness as due to its estrangement from a perfection of life, which ought to be its own but which in this world of conflicting motives and transient activities seems hopelessly remote. Whether you express your unhappy consciousness in purely skeptical or in devout form, that is, with emphasis upon a cynical or upon a mystical attitude, is to a certain degree a matter of accident. But of course the devotional expression is the deeper one and looks more in the direction in which the solution of the problem, according to Hegel, is to be found. The unhappy consciousness is therefore depicted in its religious form, and with a constant use of metaphors derived from mediæval Christianity. In fact Hegel is here unquestionably treating one aspect of the religious consciousness. It is however very notable, and characteristic of the method of the *Phaenomenologie* that Hegel does not regard this form of consciousness as a genuine expression of religion in its wholeness. Religion as such appears in the *Phaenomenologie* as a social and not as an individual life. The unhappy consciousness is here expressly what William James would call a variety of religious experience; it is not a concrete form of religion. It may appear in connection with the most various phases of faith. Viewed, so to speak, metaphysically, it involves a distinctly individual interpretation of one's relation to the universe. That which the unhappy consciousness seeks, can therefore indeed be named God. It might also be named just Peace, or the Ideal Self.

If the unhappy consciousness occurs to a person at a given phase, he will of course use the terminology of his phase. But viewed as a personal experience, the unhappy consciousness is a search for tranquillity, tranquillity won by some union between the individual and his own ideal, between the lower and the higher self. The unhappy consciousness, then, is what James has described as the vague consciousness of being out of harmony with the higher powers, while these higher powers constitute, after all, very much what James characterizes as one's subliminal self. Hegel, who knows not the modern psychological vocabulary, calls this subliminal self with which the unhappy consciousness is out of harmony its own conceived and long-sought "changeless consciousness," or as he briefly puts it, "the Changeless." In other words, in this particular incarnation, the *Weltgeist* of whom we spoke at the last time, is seeking himself through some lonely type of religious devotion. His world is nothing but himself; and he is so far indeed idealistic.

He is not thinking of nature or of fortune or of other people or of society. He is brooding. He is thinking only of his own soul and its salvation. The divine that he pursues is only the blessed relief from his sorrow which he seeks through his devotions. In brief, his religion is a phantasy of his inner consciousness, although his social relations to some real existing church may indeed give a deeper significance to the process than he alone can recognize. He himself is shut up in the cell with his sorrows and his ideals. But his difficulty is that he seems wholly self-estranged and foreign to himself.

Hegel depicts this form of individual self-consciousness with a rather excessive detail but with a very profound insight into the sentimentality, the hopelessness, and the genuine meaning of the entire process. The dialectic situation depends upon the pathetic fact that the unhappy consciousness always actually has its salvation close at hand, but is still forbidden by its own presuppositions to accept that salvation. What it seeks is nothing whatever but an inner self-confidence, which it apparently ought to win by a mere resolution—an act of manly will. Yet, by hypothesis, it is estranged from every resolute inner self-consciousness, since it conceives all good solely as belonging to its object, the Changeless. It prays to the Changeless, it longs for the Changeless. It tries to see its Lord face to face. But it always finds, says Hegel, only the empty sepulchre whence the Lord has been taken away. "Nay, if I find the Holy Grail itself, it too will fade and crumble into dust."

Under these circumstances, however, the consciousness in question does indeed learn to make a transition, which is in so far positive and which is due to taking over the lesson that the slave learned from the master. After all,

the very emptiness of the sepulchre shows that if the
Lord is not here he is arisen. Seek not the living among
the dead. One's seeking must become an activity;
one must do something even as the risen Lord does. And
so the mere sentiment of the first stage of this unhappy
consciousness changes into service. But the service is not
a control of natural phenomena; it is not essentially any
social business. It is the doing of what is pleasing in the
sight of the Changeless; it is the life of self-sacrifice as
such—the self-chastisement of the devotee. But once
more the division recurs. What is done is, after all, but
the transient deed of a poor sinner. The Changeless, the
perfect, cannot be realized hereby. One's work is but
vain. One's righteousness is as rags. The true self is
not satisfied. One's best work gets all its value, (when it
gets any value at all), from the fact that the foreign
and changeless self somehow kindly inspires this deed
of righteousness and permits the poor sinner to do something for his Lord. But the doer himself still remains
worthless, whatever he does. He wishes to be meet for
the master's service, but after all he is but a broken and
empty vessel, and this is all that he has to offer for the
master's service. And under these circumstances the only
hope must indeed come from the other side. After
all, the changeless self is concerned in the salvation of
this poor sinner, makes its own sacrifice for him, permits
communion with the Changeless, gradually sanctifies the
poor soul through the higher life, means in the end to
bring the imperfect into union with itself. *Quantus labor
ne sit cassus,* and so at length perhaps, through self-dis-
cipline, self-abnegation, endless self-chastisement, the imperfect self does come to some consciousness of a new
and sanctified and redeemed nature. The Changeless

perchance has come to live in it. It has now become, through the ineffable grace of the Changeless, the instrument of the divine.

But hereupon, for the unhappy consciousness the enemy appears, as Hegel says, in his worst form. The former self-abnegation changes into spiritual pride. The sanctified person becomes the home of vanity, and needs a constantly renewed casting down into the depths of humility, until this very pride in its own expertness in the art of self-humiliation becomes the inspiring principle of its life. It becomes intensely overcareful as to every detail of its fortunes and of its functions. Its existence is one of painful conscientiousness, of fruitless dreariness. And yet, after all, if it could only reflect, it would see that through its despair it has already found the essential experience. For what it has essentially discovered is that if a man will reasonably submit himself to the conditions of the true life, he must attain, through activity, a genuine unity with his ideal world. In other words, the unhappy consciousness is simply seeking in its lonesomeness what the civilized man is finding in his concrete relations, not to the enemies whom he kills, nor to the slaves whom he controls, nor to the abstract ideals that he follows, but to the humane life in which he finds his place. Whenever consciousness reaches, says Hegel, a stage of genuine reason, it becomes sure of itself and rests from the vain labors of all this suspicious self-questioning. It finds indeed a new field of work, and of intense and absorbing work, but not the labor of conquering these fantastic spiritual foes. It becomes assured that the practically humane life is, in meaning, one with the whole of reality. The unhappy consciousness, however, can in and for itself never recognize this fact. It will not wake up to its own truth. To quote Hegel's words: "Rather does this consciousness only hear as if spoken by some meditating voice, the sole, fragile assurance that its own grief is in the yet hidden truth of the matter the very reverse, namely, its salvation; the bliss of an activity which rejoices in its tasks. This voice of the spirit tells the unhappy consciousness in its own way that the miserable deeds of the poor sinner are in some hidden truth the perfect work, and the real meaning of this assurance is that only what is done by an individual is or can be a deed. But for the unhappy consciousness both activity and its own actual deeds remain miserable. Its satisfaction is its sorrow and the freedom from this sorrow in a positive joy it looks for in another world, in heaven. But this other world, where its activity and being are to become and to remain its own real activity and being— what is this world but the world of the civilized reason, where consciousness has the assurance that in its individuality it is and possesses all reality?"* But this, insists Hegel, is just the normal consciousness of the civilized man. It is what one might call the form of a realistic consciousness which is also saturated by idealism. And herewith the *Weltgeist* transmigrates again into the new individual form of the man who says, "The world is mine to live in and therein to find my fulfilment and my task." This new world of youthful and vigorous consciousness, this world of the *renaissance of individuality*, Hegel calls the World of Reason, but of reason still in its individual rather than in its social expression. Thus, *Vernunft* at this stage of the *Phaenomenologie* appears as equivalent

* See the author's translation of this section of the *Phenomenology* under the title "The Contrite Consciousness," in Benjamin Rand's *Modern Classical Philosophers*, pp. 614-628.—ED.

to the civilized consciousness of the man of the world or, at any rate, of the man who has a world of his own. The devotee as an individual may always remain in his cloister, but the *Weltgeist* transmigrating awakens in new individual form, as the Faust transformed by magic into the youthful seeker of good fortune, as the vigorous sentimentalist who no longer broods but passionately demands satisfaction of life, as the reformer who will transform all things into the likeness of his own ideal; in brief, as a man who has found his task and to whom the world is in the larger sense his business.

LECTURE VIII.

THE DIALECTICAL PROGRESS OF HEGEL'S
PHAENOMENOLOGIE.

AT the last lecture, in following Hegel's *Phaenomenologie des Geistes,* we reached the threshold of what he called the World of Reason, that
is, the world of organized self-consciousness, as distinct
from elemental or crude self-consciousness. The series of
types of human life and character in terms of which
Hegel has been trying in the previous parts of his book
to illustrate the logical evolution of the higher consciousness of humanity, has been followed, in our account,
through what one might call the stages of wholly imma-
ture individualism. We now come to the portrayal of a
higher series of types. I need not repeat what I have said
regarding the way in which these successive stages of consciousness form for Hegel at once a logically connected
series of views concerning life and reality and, when
viewed from another side, a freely chosen set of mere
illustrations of his systematic views. The curious union
of technical logic with free character study has been sufficiently characterized in the foregoing. We are now taking
the book simply as we find it, as a collection of portraits
illustrating Hegel's idealism and the steps by which we
may approach it. In this spirit I continue my exposition.
We are to see in what forms the self has to express itself
in order to reach completeness and self-possession.

LECTURES ON MODERN IDEALISM

I.

Hegel's *Weltgeist,* in the successive forms or finite lives through which, in our former lecture, we found him, as we might say, transmigrating, had learned the lesson that if the world is indeed the self, the self, on the other hand, can never learn to realize this very truth so long as it remains merely an *individual* self, cut off from organic ties with a world of social life. The self needs, demands—yes, must somehow create—a social world. The ideal hero of Hegel's *Phaenomenologie,* name him *Weltgeist,* or call him by a more familiar word, *Everyman,* has now learned this lesson through the experience which our former lecture reported. As savage or, if you please, as a sort of head-hunter, the *Weltgeist* has slain his fellows in order to prove, through risk and through conquest, that he is indeed the self. As master of slaves, this same Everyman has helplessly depended upon his own slaves to prove him the only lord of all. But the *Weltgeist* thus becomes the slave as well as the master. And as slave, the same *Weltgeist* has learned that only in service is there freedom. As stoic the well-trained hero, now utterly indifferent to mere fortune, has learned to serve only his own empty ideal, and so has indeed triumphed—but only in the void realm of mere abstract reasonableness, where after all, there is nothing definable left to do or to be. As skeptic, however, the same hero has observed the vanity of all such mere opinion; and hereupon has been transformed into the Unhappy Consciousness. In the dreary and solitary religion of this type, the experience of the merely unsocial self culminates. For as lonely religious devotee, estranged from himself, our hero has sorrowed through a comfortless lifetime in fantastic dreams of an impossible heaven of mere reconciliation and peace.

From these dreams the *Weltgeist* now awakens to a renewed youth as the lover of what men call real life. "The world is mine," he says; "but in that case let it be indeed a world. I will set out on the quest for my own happiness, sure that I have a right thereto."

> " 'Tis life of which our nerves are scant—
> " More life and fuller that we want."

The complex structure of Hegel's *Phaenomenologie* is at this point of the text entangled by the introduction of a long critical study of the problems of what Hegel calls "Reason as Observer of the World" (*Beobachtende Vernunft*). I shall wholly pass over this portion of the text, whose outcome is the thesis that the self, upon this stage, can win unity with its world not through mere observation but through action. Hereupon the self fully returns to the pragmatic point of view, realizing that it can win its self-control and its unity with its world, only through an active process.

This discovery once made, our hero arises with something of the enthusiasm that Tennyson's familiar words may here translate:

"Eager hearted as a boy when first he leaves his father's field."

And so our hero sets out to become a worldling.

II.

The types of consciousness which here immediately follow, are depicted with a marvelous union of sympathetic detail and of merciless dialectic peculiarly characteristic of Hegel. They are, one might say, renaissance types of character—ethical and not theoretical—interpreted, however, from the point of view which German romanticism had determined. Common to them all is the explicit recognition that without actively pursuing its ideal in a world of life, in a world of objective fortune, in an organized and social order, the self cannot win its own place, cannot be a self at all. Common to them all is the further fact that the self, despite this recognition, tries to center this acknowledged social world about just that individual man in whom the self, by chance, conceives itself, in each new incarnation, to be embodied. The conception of the social universe is thus, each time, characteristically that of vigorous and ambitious youth, confident that in him the absolute ideal has found an incarnation, nowhere else attained. "I will show you, O world, that you are my own," he says. Yet he speaks not as the savage. He is the civilized youth, with powers, talents, training, and a love of emulation. He must conquer his world; but he knows that he needs a world to conquer, and is so far dependent. Not the killing of his enemies, but spiritual mastery of the universe is his aim. Moreover, he has behind him, in essence although perhaps not in memory, the experience of the unhappy consciousness. A merely sentimental and lonely religion seems to him vanity. He is beyond all that. For the time, he has no religion whatever. He is not afraid of life. He sets out to win and to enjoy. He recognizes that the truth of things is the human, the social truth. But he is resolved that whatever any man can experience, possess, attain, is by right his, so far as his ideal demands such possession.

He begins this sort of life by taking form as Faust.

The Faust-ideal in question is due to so much of that poem as was at this time known to Hegel, and is not the Faust-ideal that Goethe later taught us to recognize as his own. Hegel conceives the Faust of the poem, as it was then before him, simply as the pleasure seeker longing for the time when he can say, "O moment stay, thou art so fair." The outcome of Faust's quest, as far as it goes, is for Hegel the discovery that the passing moment will neither stay nor be fair; so that the world where one seeks merely the satisfaction of the moment, proves rather to be the foreign world of a blind necessity. This necessity, in the guise of cruel fate, ruthlessly destroys everything that has seemed, before the moment of enjoyment, so entrancing. Pleasure seeking means, then, the death of whatever is desirable about life; and Hegel foresees, for Faust himself, so far as just his incarnation of the *Geist* can go, no escape from the fatal circle. At all events, the self is not to be found in this life of lawless pursuit of that momentary control over life which is conceived as pleasure. Such is Hegel's reading of the first part of Faust. He entitles the sketch, "Pleasure and Destiny."

The next form or incarnation of our hero is entitled, "The Law of the Heart." In making the transition from the pleasure-seeking consciousness with its inevitable discovery of a world of blind necessity, where every pleasure fades, Hegel shows a very fine comprehension of tendencies which the romantic movement had already notably exemplified, and which it was, in later literature, still further to exemplify. For the lesson of the defeated and romantic pleasure seeker's experience is indeed not, in strong and free natures, mere repentance, nor yet a mere reversion to the "unhappy consciousness." Hegel does not send his disillusioned worldling back to the cloister. The lesson rather is the discovery that the hero had been really seeking, not pleasure as such at all, but something so potent, so full of appeal to his heart that he would be as ready to die as to live for such an ideal; something in brief that could fill him with enthusiasm and devotion. The emptiness of the pleasure seeker's outcome lies simply in the fact that, after all, he has so far failed to find the "God stronger than I am, who coming shall rule over me"—that God of whom Dante tells us in the *Vita Nuova.* Let him merely define, at the moment of his disillusionment, this his deeper need, and then he becomes conscious of what his blundering quest had all the time meant. His repentance will then be no mere terror of perdition. Years after the appearance of the *Phaenomenologie,* Byron, who had tested the fate of the pleasure seeker to its end, wrote the *Stanzas to Augusta,* and his lyric after landing in Greece. Both are perfect recognitions of what Hegel here calls "the law of the heart," as the true lesson of the pleasure seeker's failure. Both express the discovery that, after pleasure has been drained to the dregs and life has so far turned into an iron necessity of failure, one still may rejoice to find out that one had all the while simply been looking for a way to fill one's heart full of a sovereign love for something worthy of one's faith:

> " And if dearly that error hath cost me,
> And more than I once could foresee,
> I have found that, whatever it lost me,
> It could not deprive me of *thee.*
> From the wreck of that past, which hath perish'd,
> Thus much I at least may recall,

192

It hath taught me that what I most cherish'd
Deserved to be dearest of all:
In the desert a fountain is springing,
In the wild waste there still is a tree,
And a bird in the solitude singing,
Which speaks to my spirit of *thee.*"

III.

This transformation of the love of pleasure into the
longing for a passionate ideal, is something much deeper
than mere remorse. The outcome of the search for the
satisfying moment of experience is the discovery of the
law that all passes away and turns into the sere and yel-
low leaf. The lesson is that if one adopts this very law
as one's own, if one scorns delight and lives laborious
days, simply because all else fades, while the inmost desire of the heart may outlast all transient contentment,
then one is nearer to one's own true expression. Choose
your ideal then, choose it anyhow, and be ready to die
for it. Then for the first time you learn how to live. Living means having something dear enough to fill the heart.

Thus Hegel suggests his diagnosis of the remarkable
transition from passionate pleasure seeking to vehement
self-surrender which is so notable in romantic periods
and in youthful idealism.

The next type, the hero of the "law of the heart," hereupon appears as an enthusiast for an ideal—what ideal
is indeed indifferent except so far as his own mere feeling is his guide. His heart tells him that this *is* his ideal.
He is ready to die for it. That is enough. He has found
himself. All about him, of course, is the vain world of
the people who do not comprehend this ideal. But the

hero is an altruist. His heart beats high for the good of mankind. What mankind needs is to learn of his ideal. He is therefore a reformer, a prophet of humanity, one of whom, as his own heart infallibly tells him, the world is not worthy. He is good enough, nevertheless, to be ready to save this so far ruined world. Meanwhile, the ideal for which he fights is always essentially sentimental. If as reformer he wins his triumph, he instantly discovers that whatever has won the day has by the very triumph been turned into mere worldliness; and he is even more disposed to quarrel with his party, so soon as it has triumphed, than he had been to condemn the base world as it was before he came into it. Nothing, therefore, is less to his mind than a cause which has triumphed; such a cause is no longer a mere affair of the heart. The romantic reformer lives by having a base world to condemn. He would indeed reform it; but woe unto the social order that chances to accept his reform. His heart is too pure to be content with such humdrum worldly actuality. He rages because the base world has profaned the ideal even through the very act of pretending to accept it.

Since in a similar fashion all other hearts, if once awakened, are laws unto themselves, the realm of such a company of romantic reformers is a renewal, upon a higher level, of the primal warfare of all against all. It is a world of mad prophets, each the fool of his own vanity. In depicting this type, Hegel has in mind the speech of the hero of Schiller's *Robbers,* and the enthusiasts of storm and stress literature generally, in so far as they are humanitarian in their pretences and anarchical in their conflict with the prevailing social order. The portrayal of the type is merciless in its dialectic, but is not without its obvious justice.

IV.

To the tragi-comedy of the purely sentimental reformers, succeeds the more familiar comedy of the romantic
knight-errants—the heroes whose ideal has dropped
the passionate insistence upon a sentimental dream,
and has assumed the form of a coherent law, but
who still center this law of the world about their own
noble personalities. Here, as is obvious, Hegel is dealing
with that type whose dialectic Cervantes had long since
rendered classic. It is necessary for Hegel, however, to
incorporate a representative of this type into his own
series; and he does so very briefly, but effectively. The
hero of knightly virtues here depicted is no longer
a mediæval figure, and the portrait is not directly that
of Don Quixote. The illusions in question take only such
forms as belong to Hegel's own age. In essence, the attitude depicted is that of the ideally minded youthful
altruist whose knightly quest is directed against the lawless selfishness which, in his opinion, infests the social
order, while the knightly character itself takes pride, not
indeed like the foregoing type, in mere chance enthusiasms, but in its steadily loyal attitude of self-sacrifice
for its chivalrous purpose. It defines its ideal as virtue
in the abstract, as nobility of character. All of its natural
powers are to be disciplined, not for the sake of enforc-
ing the law of the heart, but for the sake of overcoming
the wicked ways of the world where selfishness reigns.
The natural man is now denounced as a brutish self-
seeker. The world as it is contains giants of wrongdoing,
and is given over to selfishness. The knightly soul is opposed to the natural man and fights for the cause of an
ideal chivalry whose essence consists in loving and serv-

ing virtue and surrendering one's self with no more organized purpose than that of such self-surrender.

The admirable personal intents of such an idealist do not blind us to the fact that, as Hegel points out, his powers and his culture are due to the very society that his lofty conceit affects to despise. And since in his plans he now lacks any definite relation to the objective demands of this real social order, since it is not good citizenship which guides his activities, but simply his own impression regarding the nobility of his character and aims, his ideal has to remain not merely unpractical, but empty. He lives in phrases and illusions. As against his boasts, it is the selfish world after all that, in its own crude way, accomplishes whatever social good is accomplished at all.

V.

The result of the dialectic of these successive types is so far obvious. The individual in order to come to himself needs a world, and a social one, to win over and to control. But control can only be won through self-surrender. Hence the individual needs a world where he may find something to which he can devote himself as to an objective truth—something quite definite which he can serve unhesitatingly so as to be free from the querulousness of the restless reformer, and free too from the idle vanity of the knight-errant. The true world must become for me the realm of my life task, of my work, of my objectively definite and absorbing pursuit. Only so can I truly come to myself and to my own. Is not then, after all, the artist who pursues art for art's sake, the scholar, who loves learning just for learning's sake, the man, in brief, who is completely given over to a laborious calling just for the sake of the absorbing consciousness which accompanies this calling—is not such a man, at length, in possession of the true form of self-consciousness? My work, my calling, my life task—this I pursue not because I wish for mere pleasure, but because I love the work. Moreover, this task is indeed the law of my heart; but I do not seek to impose it upon all other men. I leave them free to choose their life tasks. Nor is my calling merely an object of sentiment. I view it as a worthy mode of self-expression. Meanwhile, unlike the knight-errant, I do not pretend to be the one virtuous representative of my calling, who as such is reforming the base world. No, in my calling, I have my colleagues who work with me in a common cause. This cause (*die Sache*) is ours. Here, then, are the conditions of an ideal society. Here subject and object are at least, it might seem, upon equal terms. We who pursue a common calling exist as servants of our *Sache;* and this cause—our science, our art, our learning, our creative process, whatever it be—this exists by virtue of our choice, and of our work. Meanwhile, if this is not your calling, you must not ask, as from without, what this "cause" of ours is good for. Our art is just for art's sake; our learning is its own reward. Our cause is indeed objective; we serve it; we sacrifice for it; but it is its own excuse for being. If you want to attain the right type of self-consciousness, find such a cause, make it yours, and then serve it.

The phase of consciousness suggested lies very near to the mind of a scholar such as Hegel; near also to the thoughts of the artists and the students of a time such as his. Beyond pleasure seeking, beyond the sentimental scheming of reforms, beyond youthful knight-errantry, lies a type of self-consciousness with which many a strong man has long been content. This type involves a calm love of a definite calling, which seems to be pursued unquestioningly and just for its own sake. What does one want, after all, but just an absorbing life task? So to live is to find the self which is also an universe.

In explaining the dialectic of this type of consciousness Hegel shows all the skill of the reflective man who is confessing the only too natural defects incident to his own calling. And no reader can doubt the thoroughness of the confession. For no sentimental dreamer of the foregoing romantic types fares worse under Hegel's dissection than does the type of the scholar or the artist who defines the self in terms of the "cause," and who thereupon can say nothing better of the "cause" than that it is its own excuse for being. Such an ideal Hegel finds wholly accidental and capricious, and shrewdly notes that what the scholars and artists in question really mean by their pretended devotion to the "cause" is that they are fond of displaying their wits to one another and of showing their paces and of winning applause, and with a touch of the old savagery about them are also fond of expressing contempt for the failures of other men. The actual behavior of these devotees of the cause is described in paragraphs of a characteristically dry humor. The learned author or the confident artist, vain of his toilsome scholarly or creative task, first puts all his powers into it; then feels sure, in his own mind, that this is indeed a great piece of work, since, after all, the self is in it; and hereupon, with an elaborate display of modesty, he solemnly explains in his preface or in letters to his friends that he knows how little he has done. Yes, he has done a mere nothing. He has only wished to show, by his poor essays, his devotion to the cause, of which he is but the humblest of servants.

Such is his honorable way of appearing objective. Hereupon, like flies, the critics settle upon the now publicly
visible work. They too protest their devotion to the cause.
Wholly in its service, and of course not because of their
condescending vanity, nor yet because of their own ill-
suppressed but malicious glee, they either loftily praise
and approve, or else, if they can, tear to pieces the
worthy or unworthy work. Of course the author listens
disenchanted. And of such is the kingdom of those who
have no justification for their life task except that it is
a life task. What they are busy in pleasing, is their own
vanity. They merely call it an objective task.

Hegel's title, prefixed to his sketch of this type of consciousness, sufficiently summarizes his view. It runs:
*"Das geistige Thierreich und der Betrug, oder die Sache
selbst."* We may freely translate: "The Intellectual
Animals and their Humbug; or the Service of the
Cause." Few more merciless sketches of the pedantry
and hypocrisy that may take on the name of objectivity
and of devotion, have ever been written. For Hegel had
grown up *im geistigen Thierreich* amongst the intellectual animals and he knew them to the core.

VI.

Yet, once again, the result of this dialectic is positive.
The ideal of the intellectual animals is in fact a sound
one. Their hypocrisy lies merely in pretending to have
found this ideal in art for art's sake, or in learning for
learning's sake. Suppose that there indeed is a task
which is not arbitrarily selected by me as my task, and
then hypocritically treated as if it were the universal
task which I impersonally serve. Suppose that the genuine task is one forced upon us all by our common nat-

ural and social needs. This then will be *"die Sache,"* our work, our life, whether we individually admit the fact or no. Against the magnitude of this common task, the individual's service will then indeed be as nothing, and the individual, when he notes this, may frankly admit the fact without any hypocritical posing. On the other hand, this task will furnish for each man his only possible true self-expression in terms of human action. Is there such a task, such a *Sache?* Hegel replies in effect: Yes, the consciousness of a free people, of a *Volk,* of an organized social order, will constitute such an expression of selfhood. To each of its loyal citizens, the state whose life is that of such a people will be his objective self. This his true self then assigns to the individual his private task, his true cause, gives dignity and meaning to his personal virtues, fills his heart with a patriotic ideal, and secures him the satisfactions of his natural life. Here at last in this consciousness of a free people, we have— no longer crude self-consciousness, no longer lonely seeking of impossible ideals, and no longer the centering of the world about the demands of any one individual. In this consciousness of a free people each individual self is in unity with the spirit of the entire community. And herewith the world of the *Geist* begins. All the previous forms were abstractions, fragments of life, bits of selfhood. In history they appear as mere differentiations within some form of the life of the *Geist*—as mere phases of individual life which involve, as it were, a sleep and a forgetting of the unity upon which all individual life is based. An organized social order is the self for each one of its loyal subjects. The truth of the individual is the consciousness of the people to which he loyally belongs.

The pathos of these words, written as they were at a moment when Hegel himself was very much a man without a country and when already the invader's heel was on the soil of Germany, suggests to us that the *Geist* also, thus hopefully introduced, is to have its dialectical experiences, and its forms of disillusionment. As a fact, the tale of the *Geist* is more of a tragedy than is that of the individual life.

\ The first type of the *Geist* is that of the small but already highly developed state, as was, for instance, the ideal Grecian commonwealth—so small that its citizens feel near to one another, while this state is so highly developed as to value its own freedom and to demand definite loyalty from every subject.

The problem of such a social order, as of every social order, is of course the maintaining of the equilibrium between individual rights and social duties. This is for Hegel simply the problem of subject and object in its social form. The commonwealth is conscious in and through its individuals; but they, as loyal subjects, view themselves as its expression and instrument. So each of the two members of this relation, the consciousness of the commonwealth and that of the individual, may in turn be regarded as the true subject and as the true object of the social world. As in Schelling's doctrine of the self, however, the relation involved proves to be unsymmetrical and hence, in each finite form, unstable.

In the ideal small commonwealth, however, the problem as to the relation between the individual and the social order does not yet appear as a direct conflict between the personal rights of one who is in the modern sense a free citizen, and the public rights of the government. For in this stage the loyal individual is, in ideal at least, essentially devoted to the filling of his social station whatever that is. He has conscious rights only by virtue of this station. The modern notion of individual rights is a much later evolution. Hegel uses as his illustration of this form of social consciousness, not the literal history of the Grecian commonwealth (for that is clouded, he thinks, by accidental motives), but rather the ideal view of a commonwealth which he finds presented in the Greek heroic tragedy—especially in the Œdipus trilogy of Sophocles. It is notable that at the moment we are reminded of an essentially analogous situation by what we nowadays hear of the social ideals of old Japan,* where individual rights were apparently conceived wholly in terms of social station.

In such an ideal commonwealth—the ideal heroic social order of the Greek tragedy—or the analogous ideal of old Japan, the antithesis between the individual and the social order is represented by the conflict between family piety and the demands of the existing rulers of the state. In other words, the social order here exists in a two-fold form, as the family and as the government. The family interest here centers, however, about its devotion to its dead. The individual, while living, is friend or foe of the state, and has value for society only as such. But as a dead member of the family, the individual has absolute rights, which are recognized through funeral ceremonies and through ancestor worship. Hence the possibility of a conflict between family piety and the demands of the state—a conflict upon which the tragedy of Antigone is based. Hegel illustrates the conflict at length, in the form

* A remarkable illustration of this *Gestalt* is contained in ''The Story of the Forty-Seven,'' in *Tales of Old Japan,* collected by A. B. Mitford.—Ed.

which might appear trivial in its detail were not a reader of our day reminded, by what he hears of Japan, of the manifold ways in which patriotism and family honor, the duties of daily life and the reverence for the dead, seem there to have stood in various antitheses and to have involved tragic conflicts. The essence of such tragedies, according to Hegel, is that loyalty is divided in twain, into loyalty to the underworld—shadowy, mysterious, but absolute—and loyalty to the visible government, whose commands are explicit, but are of today. The laws of the underworld are socially binding. They are not of today or of yesterday. No man knows whence they came. But the visible social order is insistent and authoritative. One can resist it only by a deed which involves fault. That such fault must occur, even when the wrongdoer is innocent of any but the most loyal intention—this is the Fate of this stage of social consciousness, and is typified by the tragic fault of one who, like Œdipus unwittingly slays his father, and weds his own mother, but who even thereby becomes the ruler of the state; and is again typified by the deliberate yet fatally necessary fault of Antigone, who with womanly piety takes sides with the underworld and performs her duty to her dead brother in defiance of the will of the ruler.

In brief, the ideal commonwealth lives through an unconsciousness as to what its own inner doubleness of loyalty means. It is unstable. Its only resource is in exercising its loyalty through active conflict with other states. But warfare breaks down the simpler form of society, and inevitably leads over to the next great stage of social development—the stage of Imperialism.

The imperial social order is one in which the antithesis of public and of private rights is explicit and is deliberately adjusted through a system of laws. The ideal purpose of these laws is to secure to every man his own, while the laws themselves are administered by a sovereign power, the state. The state, no longer a commonwealth whose dignity is instinctively recognized, a social order to which loyalty is a natural and inevitable tribute, needs to be symbolized to the eyes of the subject by the definite will of an individual, the personal sovereign. The first conflict is now between his will, which as the will of an individual is arbitrary, and his true vocation, which is to enforce just laws, securing thereby to every subject property and personal rights. A second conflict appears between his will and the equally arbitrary will of a subject. Family piety gives place to militarism. One has duties no longer to the dead, but solely to the living. Justice is the ideal; but arbitrary enactment is the fact. And the conflict, as fatal as it was in the original social order, is no longer the mysterious conflict between the underworld and the visible authorities. It is the explicit conflict of law and order on the one hand, caprice and accident on the other. In this conflict the sovereign and his subjects are equally involved. The state is at once a necessity and an oppression to all. Nobody can either permanently endure any one form of government or do without it. In the imperial world the spirit thus exists estranged from itself, but bound nevertheless to live and to develop through this estrangement. It is essentially a social mind, but is also a social mind whose expressions are as unstable as they are mighty.

The one resource of the spirit, under these conditions, is self-cultivation—the education of the civilized consciousness to a full comprehension of the problems of the social order. We need not undertake to follow here the stages through which, in Hegel's account, this education of the social mind passes. The forms of cultivated individualism heretofore discussed are themselves phases of consciousness which arise in the course of this training. The skeptical discovery that the state appears to exist simply as the embodiment of the selfish will of its subjects, and that loyal professions are mere cloaks for individual greed, the growth of a corrupt use of political power even by virtue of the growth of the general social intelligence, the conflict of the social classes—these are phases in the great process of the cultivation which the social mind gives to itself. These phases culminate in the consciousness which the Enlightenment of the eighteenth century represents. Society is indeed necessary, but it exists solely for the sake of forming, nourishing, and cultivating, free individuals. Utility is the sole test of social truth. All that is real exists simply in order to make men happy. Whatever principle underlies this world-process is an unknowable Supreme Being. Visibly true is only this, that what tends to the greatest good of the greatest number of individual men is alone justified. This, then, is what we have been seeking. This is wisdom's last social word. Away with all arbitrary laws and sovereign powers. Away with loyalty to anything but the common rights of all men. We are all free and equal. The *Geist* has been transformed into the multitude of free and equal individuals. Let the people come to their own.

Herewith, then, comes the Revolution, the absolute freedom—and the Terror. For the horde of individuals thus let loose are whatever they happen to be. The will of all is indeed to be done. But who shall do it? The sovereign ruler? But the sovereign is dead. The representatives of the people? But these are now free individuals, with no loyalty that they can any longer define in rational terms. The only way for them to become conscious of the universal will is to express their own will. They mean of course to do whatever brings the greatest happiness to the greatest number. But they have now no test of what is thus to be universally useful except what is furnished by the light of their own personal experience. Their subjective decision they therefore impose upon all others. Thus they become a faction, appear as public enemies, and are overthrown. Society has returned to primitive anarchy, and exists once more as the war of all against all.

VII.

The *Geist,* so far, has failed to find, in the literal social world, in the political realm, any stable union of its subjective and objective aspects. The lesson is, not that the old individualism was right, but that the true social order needs a higher embodiment. In the literal political world, the *Geist* is indeed able, in Hegel's opinion, to take care of its own, so far as the conditions will permit. It will not tolerate anarchy. It will resume some type of relatively stable social constitution. But here, after all, it has no abiding city.

The "empire of the air" remains, however, still to conquer. And Hegel hereupon depicts, in terms derived from Kant and Fichte, what he now calls the moral theory of the universe of the spirit. Upon this stage the mind, still aware of its essentially social destiny, now undertakes to define the reality as a certain eternal and ideal order which is valid for all rational beings—the city of God, whose constitution never passes away. This higher and eternal realm, where the moral autonomy of every free agent is guaranteed even by virtue of his acceptance of a moral law that he conceives as binding for all rational beings, is as true as it is shadowy and full of antitheses. On earth this ideal moral order can never be realized, for on earth we see only phenomena. Only the noumenal free moral agents, whose dwelling lies beyond time and space and beyond phenomena, can create that city of God and can consciously dwell therein. Yet we mortals have worth only in so far as, by our deeds, we actually take part in the creation of that perfect moral order. The real universe—this moral realm—the divine order that lies beyond sense, will infallibly ensure the triumph of this absolute right, whatever we poor mortals do. Yet we are free moral agents precisely in so far as the universe needs our free and loyal deeds in order to aid in the triumph of the right. Unless we are free moral agents, the moral world has therefore no meaning. But *if* we are free agents, then we can sin and so can endanger the triumph of the right.

Such is a suggestion of the paradox of one who tries to solve our problem by conceiving the true triumph of morality as belonging to a wholly supersensuous world. The city of God is in vain defined as merely a city out of sight. The self in vain seeks its expression in a world of which, by hypothesis, it must remain totally unconscious, so long as it remains human. The Kantian-Fichtean *moralische Weltanschauung* is thus but a fragment of the truth, a higher and social form of the "unhappy consciousness," which seeks its fulfilment in another world.

But still another form of this moral theory of reality remains. Perhaps the spirit is actually realized not through what we accomplish, but by the simple fact that, on the highest levels we intend to be rational. Perhaps the readiness is all. Perhaps the triumph of the self in its world simply takes the form of a ceaseless determination, in spite of failure and of finitude, to *aim* at the highest, at complete self-expression, at unity. Perhaps the curtain is the picture; perhaps the will is the deed; and perhaps in the end the spirit, like a higher sort of "intellectual animal," contents itself with merely saying, "I have accomplished nothing, but at least I have tried my best." So to conceive the solution is to take the position of some of Hegel's contemporaries, to whom, as formerly to Lessing, the search for the truth is all that can be viewed as accessible or as really worthy. This, in fact, is curiously near to Hegel's own form of Absolutism; but is also curiously remote from it.

For if, at last, it is the pure intent to be reasonable that constitutes reasonableness, if the whole life of the spirit, individual and social, exists only as an aim, an idea, an attitude, a purpose, still one has to remember, as one looks back over this long story of error and defeat, that every deed in which the self was expressed was, in its measure, a falling away from its own intent— was an expression of illusion, was a finite mistake, and, if conscious, was a sin against the ideal.

What consciousness so far learns, then, is that finite defect, error, sin, contradiction, is somehow of the very nature of the self, even when the self seeks and means the highest. Every effort to find and to express the perfect self is *ipso facto* a lapse into imperfection. The pure self cannot be expressed without impurity. The rational self cannot be expressed without irrationality. The absolute purpose, to be the self and to be one with one's own world, is realizable only through a continual inner conflict and a constant transcending of finite failures.

To see this, however, is also to see that it is not in the failures themselves, but in the transcending of them that the true life of the spirit—of the self—comes to be incorporated. And Hegel here expresses this by saying that it is not the consciousness of sin but the consciousness of the forgiveness of sin that brings us to the threshold of understanding why and how the true self needs to be expressed, i.e., through a process of the conscious overcoming of the defects of its own stages of embodiment, through a continual conquest over self-estrangements that are meanwhile inevitable, but never final.

To give this very view of the nature of the self, and of the relation between perfection and imperfection, finitude and the infinite—to give this view a genuine meaning, we must turn to that still higher form of the social consciousness which is historically embodied in religion.

VIII.

Religion may be defined, so Hegel says, as the consciousness of the Absolute Being. In other words religion is not, like the foregoing, the effort of one who beginning with his own individual self-consciousness as the center of his universe, tries to find the place of this individual self in his world. Religion is rather the consciousness which is seeking to express what the Absolute Being, the universe, really is, although, to be sure, religion is inevitably an interpretation of the Absolute Being as seen from the point of view of the inquiring self.

In history, religion has appeared as an attitude of the social consciousness towards the world. Religion is, for Hegel, an interpretation of the world by the social self, and by the individual man only in so far as he identifies himself with the social self. That is, the nation or the church or humanity has a religion. The individual man comes to a consciousness of his religion through his community with his nation or his church or with humanity. Religion as a purely private and personal experience could only consist of such forms as the unhappy consciousness has already exemplified.

The early forms of religion define the universe in terms of powers of nature. The unconscious idealism of the primitive mind appears in the fact that these powers tend from the outset to be conceived as living powers, which, in order that they may be viewed as sufficiently foreign and mysterious, are often typified by animals. Gradually the consciousness grows that human activity is needed in order that by suitable monuments, by vast constructions due to the worshippers themselves, the nature of the world-fashioning intelligence may be at once fittingly honored and, through imitation, portrayed. The result is seen in the vast architectural religion of Egypt, of whose true nature Hegel, when he wrote this book, had indeed small knowledge. Greek religious thought, conceiving its deities in human form, came nearer to a knowledge of the true relation of the Absolute and the finite being. The result was the religion of art, wherein the divine is portrayed by representing ideal types of human beings. But art, in humanizing the divine, inevitably tends also to humanize itself. In tragic poetry the gods gradually give place to mortal heroes; and poetry becomes consciously an imitation of human life. Comedy completes the process of this humanization. Man, who started to portray the gods, portrays, and in the end mercilessly criticizes, merely men; and the ancient religion dissolves itself in a humanistic skepticism. There are no gods. There are only men. The individual selves are all. This is the anarchical stage of religion.

But the world itself remains—mysterious, all-powerful, objective, the dark realm that this skepticism cannot pierce. The mythical personifications have turned into human fancies. Man remains on one side, the Absolute on the other. The one is self-conscious; but the other is the hidden source of self-consciousness, hopeless, baffling, overwhelming in its vastness. What form of conception can portray the now seemingly impenetrable essence of this Absolute, from which we creatures of a day seem to be now sundered as mere outer shells of meaningless finitude?

There remains one form of the religious consciousness untried. It is, at this point in human history, ready to come to life. In a highly dramatic passage Hegel now depicts how about the birthplace of this new form of consciousness there gather, like the wise men from the East, some of the most significant of the *Gestalten* so far represented: Stoicism is there, proclaiming the dignity of the self as the universal reason, but knowing not who the self is; the unhappy consciousness is there, seeking its lost Lord; the social spirit of the ancient state is there, lamenting the loss of its departed spirit: all these forms wait and long for the new birth. And the new birth comes thus: That it is the faith of the world that the Absolute, even as the Absolute that was hidden, has now revealed itself as an individual man, and has become incarnate.

This faith then holds not that an accidental individual man is all, but that the essential Absolute reveals itself as man, and this is the first form of the Christian consciousness.

This form too must pass away. This visible Lord must be hidden again in the heavens. For sense never holds fast the Absolute. There remains the consciousness, first that the Spirit of God is ever present in his church, and then that the church knows—although indeed under the form of allegories—how the Absolute Being is complete in himself only in so far as he expresses himself in a world which endlessly falls away from him into finitude, sin, darkness, and error, while he as endlessly reconciles it to himself again, living and suffering in individual form in order that, through regaining his union with his own Absolute Source, he may draw and reconcile all things to himself.

This, says Hegel, is the allegory of which philosophy is the truth.

LECTURE IX.

HEGEL'S MATURE SYSTEM.

THUS far, in our studies of Schelling's and of Hegel's early works, we have been illustrating the rise and, as one might say, the youth of the idealistic movement. We have examined some of the motives and methods of this youthful period of idealism; we have contended with some of its difficulties. We have seen some of the relations of the philosophers to the civilization of that age. We must now make an attempt to indicate the form in which philosophical idealism reached its first maturity in the system of Hegel.

I.

After Hegel published the *Phaenomenologie des Geistes,* he was for some years forced by the political consequences of the battle of Jena to abandon his work as a teacher of philosophy. He continued, however, his efforts to formulate his system, and in 1812 began the publication of his *Logik.* Not until 1816 was he able to begin work as professor of philosophy at Heidelberg. In 1818 he passed over to Berlin, where his career was continued until his death in 1831. It was at Berlin that he soon became the recognized leader of a school; and for years his philosophy had an almost overwhelming prominence in the universities of Germany.

The completed system of Hegel was outlined, during

213

his life, in his systematic treatise called the *Encyclopaedie der philosophischen Wissenschaften*. Here he appears as one attempting, like a modern Aristotle, the task of surveying the total result of human knowledge with reference to its unification in terms of an idealistic philosophy.

It will be of interest to consider briefly in what spirit Hegel attempted this unification. You well know, by this time, the main conditions which an idealistic philosopher must have in mind in such an undertaking. For an idealist the field of human knowledge is, as you will remember, no mere report of the structure of a world that exists in itself, apart from all our knowledge. On the contrary, our knowledge, whatever else it is, is an expression of ourselves. It is a revelation of the true nature of the human reason. If such an idealistic philosophy succeeds in giving an account of the universe, it will therefore show that our human reason is in unity with the ultimate nature of things. That is, it will teach that this human reason is itself the embodiment, in various individual lives, processes, investigations, practical activities, opinions, theories—the embodiment, I say, of an Absolute Reason, while the world is the creation of this Absolute. The outcome of the *Phaenomenologie* has already indicated to us how, in Hegel's view, this embodiment of an Absolute Reason in the form of our human consciousness is to be interpreted. Let us review this outcome sufficiently to see how the resulting system of philosophy must be expressed, in case such a system is possible at all.

The first result of the *Phaenomenologie* which here concerns us is the thesis that human error and human finitude are themselves a necessary part of the expression of the absolute truth. To assert this thesis is characteristic of Hegel's form of idealism, and the whole system centers about this proposition. The proposition itself is identical with the assertion that the dialectical method is the true method of philosophy. When you begin to philosophize, you seek, very properly, to escape from errors and to find the truth just as it is. Hence errors, defective points of view, false opinions, seem to you simply regrettable incidents which you wish to escape. When later you discover, as Kant wishes you to do, that human thought is through and through burdened with tendencies to error, that phenomena only are known to you, not pure truth, you feel as if the purpose of philosophy had wholly failed. But Hegel undertakes to show that truth can only be defined by taking account, as it were, of a certain necessary totality of defective or erroneous points of view. Or again, Hegel's account of the world might be defined as an assertion that the necessary and unified totality of the phenomena is itself the absolute truth; so that there is indeed no truth to seek beyond the phenomena, while nevertheless no single phenomenon, and no finite set or circle of phenomena can constitute the truth. Errors, then, are but partial views of the truth. The partiality of such views is indeed regrettable, in case you remain fast bound in and by such a partial point of view. But if you learn to view the partial truths in their setting, then you see that without the partial truths the totality of the truth would be impossible; or, in terms of the dialectical method, you see that without the errors, the truth would be impossible. As Hegel boldly expressed the situation, in the metaphorical language characteristic of his early period, and of his *Phaenomenologie,* "The truth is the Bacchanalian revel, wherein every one of the finite forms of the truth appears as an intoxicated illusion.'' (*Die Wahrheit ist der Bacchantische Taumel, worin alle Gestalten trunken sind.*) No view of the nature of truth could appear more absurd if you approach the system unsympathetically, and from without. And that is why Hegel hoped to prepare the way for his system by writing the *Phaenomenologie* as an introduction. According to this book, common sense is, as a fact, dialectical and self-refuting, since it asserts the existence of a world of fact independently of its own thoughts, while common sense is still unable to define or to describe this external world except in terms of the categories of its own thought. So far Kant's analysis inevitably brings us, as we deal with the problems that lead us over to idealism. Meanwhile, common sense, while thus theoretically at war with its own anti-idealistic conceptions, is all the while, in Hegel's opinion, practically idealistic, since every one of us naturally views the world as centered about his own personality, and conceives the nature of things pragmatically, that is, as possessing reality precisely in so far as this nature of things has value for his own conduct. Hence the common sense point of view at once says, ''The facts are the facts, whatever I may think,'' and also adds, ''What I have to conceive as true, I must regard as true; for otherwise I have no basis for action, and no plan of conduct.''

Yet common sense, self-contradictory as it is, is an absolutely inevitable beginning for philosophy. Whatever truth we are to come to see must, then, come to our knowledge through a process which involves, not the abandonment, but the supplementing of common sense—not the dropping of those errors which inevitably reassert themselves whenever we move about as we do in the world of common sense, but the enlarging of our consciousness through an insight which shows those errors to be a necessary aspect and moment of the absolute truth.

Not only is the point of view of common sense thus at once erroneous and necessary—a way to the truth, though leading through the very labyrinth where the monster of error dwells—but the same character of the truth, the same relative justification of error, has appeared at every stage of that progress of consciousness of which the *Phaenomenologie* is supposed to be the record. The series of stages of consciousness which Hegel has traced is, according to him, substantially inevitable. It is indeed not necessary that the individual man should in each case literally repeat in his personal life, the march over the long road of error through which the human race has so far found its way. That is, the individual man need not first, like the savage, kill his enemies in order to learn how self-assertion is possible only in social forms; he need not be a master or a slave, a monk, or a Faust, an anarchist or a loyal subject of an ancient Greek commonwealth, in order to learn the truth that was incorporated in each of these forms of life. But that is because, these forms of life having actually expressed their truth and having paid the penalty of their errors, each by asserting itself, and then by passing away, the individual man can learn their lesson in a more or less abstract way, and so can use this lesson in defining higher grades of insight. Hegel, however, insists that without the actual expression, in living form, of the lower type of consciousness, the higher type could not find its own expression. The essence of this higher life is to be the truth of the lower stages; and so in general it is of the essence of all truth to be the truth of some error, the

goal which that error was seeking. Hence the Absolute
exists only as the truth of the lower and of the relative;
the infinite exists only as the truth of the finite; the perfect can be real only as the fulfilment of what is sought
by the imperfect.

II.

A second result of the *Phaenomenologie* is, in Hegel's
opinion this: Since each imperfect stage of consciousness
is an interpretation of the whole real universe from some
limited or finite point of view, and since each such interpretation is led over from its own lower stage to the next
higher stage of consciousness by a process of what might
be called immanent self-criticism—a process whereby
each stage comes to a self-consciousness regarding its
own purposes and its own meaning—it follows that the
method of philosophy must consist in a deliberate and
systematic development of this very mode of self-criticism of the processes and attitudes of consciousness. In
the *Phaenomenologie* we found that Hegel simply accepted from experience the historical fact that certain
types of human character, of social life, and of religious
consciousness, exist or have existed. We found him, after
accepting from without, as it were, these forms, thereupon applying his dialectical method to each of them in
succession, and so showing how each form was dialectical
and was therefore inadequate to express its own inmost
purposes. We then found him at the close of such dialectical history of a stage of consciousness, looking about
him, as it were, in experience and in history for a form
or type of consciousness which should express some
higher phase of the truth and of insight. Such an application of the dialectical method characterized his introduction to philosophy. But herewith we found indeed

but a fragmentary expression of what, to Hegel's mind, the dialectical method must become when applied to the proper business of the philosophical system itself. The change which must characterize, for such a thinker, the transition from his introduction to his finished system, thus becomes fairly obvious.

The system of Hegel must do for our fundamental ideas of truth, for the necessary categories of the mind, and for the answering of our various questions about truth and reality, what the *Phaenomenologie* undertook to do for the various stages whereby the human mind has approached the philosophical point of view itself. Has our thought a certain necessary nature? Are our true categories only the expression of some one fundamental principle of reason? Is the nature of things an expression of the reason? Is the variety of human selves an inevitable manifestation of the one Absolute Reason? Are Nature and Mind different stages in the manifestation of this one Reason? Such, as you know, are the questions which a system of Hegel's type proposes to answer in the affirmative. And you are now prepared to understand at least in a general way, the motives which led Hegel to undertake this answer by means of a repeated and, in fact an unweariedly persistent application and reapplication of his dialectical method.

Hegel, like his predecessors, conceives the whole nature of things as due to the very principle which is expressed in the self. But now, as the *Phaenomenologie* has especially taught us, the self, in Hegel's opinion, is through and through a dialectical being. It lives by transcending and even thereby including its own lower manifestations. Every finite form that it can take exists only to be transcended, but even thereby exists to be included in the self's complete life. The self sins, but only to repent its own sin, by attaining through this very repentance a renewed moral vigor. It dies; but only to rise on stepping stones of its dead selves to higher things. It errs, in order thereby to illustrate the truth which is richer than the error. The *Phaenomenologie* has merely illustrated this general process. The mature system shall define the same process in exact and technical terms, and in these very terms shall apply the resulting conception of the self to explaining the whole world as due to the very principle which the self embodies. This, then, is Hegel's philosophical ideal.

III.

Meanwhile, as we also know, this form of idealism will undertake to deduce the variety of the categories of our thought from a single principle. And this principle, in Hegel's case, will again be the self. Consequently Hegel will attempt to show how the various fundamental conceptions which the human mind uses in the processes exemplified by the various sciences are themselves stages in the formation and in the expression of self-consciousness. These stages will be united in a series by ties of the same sort as those which, in the *Phaenomenologie*, bound together the various *Gestalten des Bewusstseins*. The various categories of our human thought, such as being, change, quality, quantity, measure, thing, property, content, form, internal, external, causality, substance—the fundamental conceptions, in brief, which we use in our various sciences as our tools for comprehending the nature of things—these will be, for Hegel, one and all of them stages in the self-expression of our thoughtful activity—*Gestalten*, as it were, of the thinker's life. Each category will be necessary in its place and for its own purpose. But no one of them, by itself, will have absolute validity, unless indeed the name for their total system, the *Idee* itself as the *Absolute Idee,* shall be viewed as itself one of these categories. Each category, each idea such as quality, quantity, etc., shall be limited—a necessary, but an abstract, and in so far as it is merely abstract, an untrue expression of the total nature of things. As the master or the slave, as the stoic or the monk, as the pleasure seeker or the intellectual animal, as each of these types both *was* and *was not* the true self, *was* the self under a limitation, but therefore *was not* the whole self, and so had to give place, in the evolution of life, to a truer *Gestalt;* so too it will prove to be the case with the categories. Each special category will be the truth, but not the whole truth of things. Each, then, will find its truth in later categories. But the last category, which will end the systematic list and which will thus close the series, will express the truth only in so far as it explicitly includes in itself the totality of all the other and previous categories; precisely as the Absolute Life, of which the close of the *Phaenomenologie* gave us a hint, exists only as differentiating itself into the totality of the finite *Gestalten,* as expressing itself in them, and so forgiving their finitude just because the wealth of its own perfection dwells in their totality.

IV.

In a way similar to that in which Hegel develops his system of categories, he must undertake also, in accordance with his principles, to deal with the problem of the nature of the real world, with the relations of the physical world and the mind, and with the origin and with the social and historical connections of those various types of personality which the *Phaenomenologie* merely accepted as empirically given facts of life, and used there merely as illustrations of stages of consciousness. In dealing with the vast range of problems thus suggested, Hegel was obviously sure to meet with the severest test of the adequacy of the philosophical conceptions whose significance we have been sketching in the foregoing. It is one thing to use examples from human life as instances of the dialectical method. It is another thing to show in detail that by means of the sole principle that the nature of the Absolute is most completely expressed in the nature of the self, one can explain the necessity that the life of the Absolute should also be expressed in such an enormous wealth of forms as those which external nature and human history present to our experience. Yet the postulates which determined Hegel's general fashion of thought, and which the foregoing account has now brought to our notice, required him to undertake, although with certain express limitations, a task of this general nature. And his courage was equal to the enterprise, so far as he was able to define to himself what this enterprise meant. It is fair, however, to note at once under what limitations and subject to what restrictions Hegel undertook his task of surveying the sum total of the results of the special sciences known to him, and of unifying these results by means of an application of the dialectical method.

It is indeed unfair to suppose that Hegel regarded as the ideal business of philosophy to deduce a priori the necessity according to which the absolute nature of things must require, in consequence of its inevitable dialectic, the existence of each individual thing in nature or even

of each law of the physical world, or of each kind of
living creature, or of each event of universal history, or
of each individual man or nation. People have often attributed to Hegel an extravagant a-priorism of this type,
according to which every finite fact should be, in all its
individual details, a necessarily required stage in the
expression of the Absolute Being. In truth, Hegel was
very far removed from such a view. It is true that he asserted that whatever has genuine actuality is an expression of the universal reason, which necessarily expresses
itself in a totality of individual infinite forms. But with
Hegel, each individual thing has a positive relation to
universal reason, and so possesses genuine actuality, not
in every respect, but only in so far as it is a *significant*
fact. It is part of what he regards as the dialectic process
of the Absolute Reason that, just as the one reason expresses itself in forms which are imperfect and finite, so,
too, it should express itself in a wealth of forms whose details are accidental as well as imperfect. The Absolute, in
order to express itself fully, must, in fact, for the very
reasons which the dialectic method emphasizes, triumph
over the unreasonable. And one way in which the unreasonable appears in experience is in the form of the accidental, of the relatively chaotic. Hegel, therefore, is
amongst the philosophers who emphasize the presence, in
the finite world, of an element of what one may call objective chance. He explicitly insists upon this fact at the
outset of his treatment of the philosophy of nature, in
the *Encyclopaedie;* and whatever one may think of this
doctrine he is profoundly unjust who attributes to Hegel
a crass literalism in the application of the famous principle: *Alles Wirkliche ist Vernünftig.* This Hegelian assertion means simply that whatever is the expression of

any essential principle, whatever, in other words, is in its detail genuinely necessary, is in the world for some good reason. That is, all true necessity is not blind but significant, is not merely fatal law but is the expression of reason. And wherever there is a good reason for the existence of any object in the world, Hegel's philosophical ideal indeed requires that philosophy shall undertake to tell what that reason is. Nevertheless, Hegel maintains upon characteristically dialectical grounds that, since reason is an active principle, finding its true place in the world as a process of conflict whereby it overcomes its own opponents, there is thus a good general reason why a great deal of what in each particular case is unreason should exist in the world to be overcome. Some of the forms of unreason we have already met with in our discussion of the *Phaenomenologie*. We have seen why Hegel thought it reasonable that such instances of unreason should occur, and should be overcome. There are, then, unreasonable facts in Hegel's world. Such are needed in order to give to Hegel's form of the reasonable principle its opportunity to triumph through its own activity. For we have seen how such triumph is significant. Hence, from Hegel's point of view, it is quite reasonable that particular instances of the irrational should be present, but to be overcome. If you hereupon consider any special instance of an unreasonable fact—a foolish sentiment, a passing mood, a particular superstition, a crime, a mob, a social catastrophe, or any one of the countless varieties of facts in the physical world—Hegel insists that such a fact, just in so far as it expresses no rational principle but is there merely as something for reason to overcome, has an element of brute chance about it, is objectively accidental. Reason requires in general that *such* facts should be found in the world, but not just *this* irrational fact. Hence philosophy has no call to "deduce" any single fact of this sort; and for Hegel such facts are legion, throughout nature and the social world. Indeed Hegel so differentiates the vocabulary which he uses to name his categories as to enable him to express the sense in which less rational types of facts have their lower and relatively accidental grade of being in his idealistic world. A well-organized social order, for instance, has what he calls *Wirklichkeit,* i.e., genuine actuality. It is, namely, the visible or phenomenal and in so far relatively adequate expression of a rational principle. But a chance phase of the social order—a panic, a mob, an audience in a theater—belongs to the world, not of actuality, but of bare existence. Hegel uses for such facts the term *Existenz;* i.e., they are not possessed of *Wirklichkeit.* So too, in the physical world, the solar system has *Wirklichkeit.* But this stone that your feet stumble over in the dark is where it is in what Hegel regards as a relatively accidental way; it is therefore merely an *existent.*

Far then from being, as commonly supposed, an extravagant rationalist, who deduced all natural and social phenomena from a single principle, so that their detail might be regarded as predictable, Hegel believed, on the contrary, that he had deduced the necessity of the objective presence of an irreducible variety of phenomena which were not further to be viewed as, in their individual detail, rational. Accordingly one may charge Hegel rather with having too hastily overlooked the possibility of discovering a deeper reasonableness in many things which now appear to us to be accidental than with having been a merely blind partisan of the reasonableness of whatever happens.

V.

Within the limits thus set, Hegel is, however, committed to the undertaking of bringing all the positive results of the sciences of his time, so far as he personally understood them, into harmony with the fundamental principles of his system. The existence of the physical world, its principal types of inorganic and of organic processes and forms, the relation between the human mind and physical nature, the general characteristics of the human mind itself, its grades and types of mental activity, the relation of the individual to society, the types of social life, the general philosophy of law, the general course of human history, the problems of religion—all the philosophical issues suggested by this catalogue of topics, Hegel undertook, in his system, to treat from his own point of view. He stands committed therefore to the attempt to show how an Absolute Being, whose inmost nature is expressed in the ways which our study has now brought to our notice, requires the presence in the world of all these various special modes of being.

The principle of the entire system whereby this result is to be obtained, is now in outline known to us. The Absolute is essentially a Self—not any one individual human self, but a completely self-determined being, of whom our varied individuality is an expression. The Absolute expresses its life in forms which, if viewed in their most general types, are identical with those categories which we have mentioned. All these expressions of the Absolute are in accordance with the principles of the dialectical method. Finite beings, as the dialectical method shows, have in themselves, in case they are viewed by a false abstraction apart from their source, a self-contradictory nature. The law of finite being is: Every finite thing in heaven and earth, when taken alone, contradicts itself, that is, illustrates what Hegel calls the *principle of negativity.* That is, again, no finite being exists in itself, or is in itself intelligible. The Infinite then, the Absolute Being, when taken in its true nature, is indeed the only reality. But the infinite, the Absolute Being, that which lies beneath and is embodied in all finite selves, cannot be taken or viewed as *merely* infinite. To view it thus would again be to contradict one's self. For so viewed it would be nothing—like the pure self of the Hindoos. The infinite, then, exists only as differentiated into the totality of its finite expressions. It is what Hegel calls the *concrete* infinite. It can *be* only in so far as it reveals, expresses, embodies, surrenders itself, and so becomes— not indeed exclusively any one finite thing, but the totality of the finite. It is beneath the finite only in so far as it is expressed in and through the finite. It is the totality of the finite viewed in its unity. The forms wherein this infinite reveals itself may still be viewed, however, first abstractly and apart from their concrete expressions. They are the categories, the necessary forms of thought. We can discover these, can develop them by means of the dialectic method; for we ourselves, not in our mere separate individuality, but in our rational consciousness as forms of the self, are identical in nature with the Absolute Being. To discover the categories is at once to define the true nature of the self, and to show how the Absolute Being, which is identical in nature with the basis of all selfhood, can alone express itself. The complete expression of the Absolute, that is, the ways in which these categories get a live expression, we find in outer nature with its wealth of forms. Each of these forms in which natural objects appear is in its essence rational; but in its special expression each natural form is finite and so is also accidental. Nature, in fact, is a phenomenal embodiment of the categories—an embodiment which exists just because the Absolute, in order to be true to its own dialectical nature, must first express itself in what appears to be an external and foreign form, even in order to win, through the conquest over this form, a consciousness of its own complete self-possession. But again, the Absolute, if viewed as conquering its natural or apparently foreign form of expression, in order thereby to win a conscious self-possession, constitutes, in contrast with external nature, the world of finite minds. A finite mind is a process whereby the Absolute expresses itself as some special instance of a conflict with nature, with chance, with the accidental. Through this conflict, through vicissitudes such as the *Gestalten* of the *Phaenomenologie* have already exemplified, the Absolute wins a consciousness of its conquest over its own self-alienation. For, as Hegel repeatedly insists, the only way in which self-consciousness can attain its goal is through such a conquest over self-alienation, through a becoming finite, through suffering as a finite being, through encountering estrangement, accident, the unreasonable, the defective, and through winning hereby a self-possession that belongs only to the life that first seeks in order to find. Assuming a natural guise, being subject to finite conditions, the Absolute wins in human form its self-possession at the moment when it comes to regard this human life as an embodiment of an absolute, that is of a divine life.

VI.

The consciousness that our natural and finite life is the mode of expression which is necessary for the very existence of an Absolute or Infinite Life takes, according to Hegel, three shapes—those of art, of religion and of philosophy. Art presents the union of the finite with the infinite by displaying a phenomenal object which directly appears as expressing an absolute ideal. Religion knows the fact of this union of the finite and the infinite in a still higher form, but expresses this knowledge in allegorical, in imaginative forms. Philosophy with the fullest consciousness of the necessary truth of the process, deduces and realizes the necessity of the existence of an Absolute Being, and the further necessity that this being should be expressed in the form, first of an active process, and then of a process which takes shape in the rational lives of conscious beings.

Art appeals to direct perception, and so involves no proof of the revelation which it actually gives of the union of finite and infinite. The proof which religion gives for its view of the unity of God and man, of absolute and of finite, takes the form of the faith of an organized body—in ancient civilization, the faith of an organized nation, in modern civilization the faith of a church. There are lower and higher forms of religion. But in any case, religion normally expresses itself in the conscious relation of a socially organized body of believers to that divine life which expresses itself to them and in them. In the religious consciousness, the Absolute Being becomes, in fact, aware of itself in and through finite conscious beings. This religious self-consciousness of the Absolute reaches its highest form in the Christian consciousness, which Hegel believed himself to be expressing with substantial accuracy.

On the other hand, the self-consciousness of the Absolute reaches its remaining and most explicit form in philosophy, where the proof of the propositions involved consists, as we have now seen, of three essential parts:

1. The general idealistic proof that thought and being, as Hegel loves to say, are identical. This means that a being whose nature is other than that which the internal necessity of a rational thinking process requires and defines, is impossible.

2. The explicit deduction of the categories which express the nature of thought, and so the ultimate nature of reality.

3. That application of the dialectical method already so largely illustrated by our study of the *Phaenomenologie*. This application proves, according to Hegel, that truth can only be expressed as a synthesis of various views which, if taken in their abstraction, are self-contradictory, while their synthesis itself is harmonious. Viewed otherwise, the same method makes clear that no finite being and no finite truth can exist or be defined in itself, and apart from the totality of truth; while, on the other hand, the infinite being, the Absolute, which is simply this totality of dialectically organized truth, can exist only as expressed in finite form.

Whenever these propositions are brought clearly and in their true synthesis into consciousness, then and there the Absolute Being, which is precisely what the self at once aims to be, and in principle is, becomes conscious of itself. The individual man who thinks becomes aware, not that his natural individuality is of any importance, in its accidental character, as a means of determining truth, but that in him the Absolute Being has become and is conscious of itself.

The philosophical and the religious consciousness, phenomenally, exist as events in time. They are expressions, however, of a process which must be viewed not as temporal but as eternal. In human philosophy and in human religion, the Absolute temporally appears as being at a certain moment what he in fact timelessly is, conscious of himself. For in the Absolute all the dialectical stages which time separates, are eternally present together.

LECTURE X.

LATER PROBLEMS OF IDEALISM AND ITS PRESENT POSITION.

IN this concluding lecture I shall indicate some of the motives which have determined the later history of idealism, and the present position of that doctrine.

I.

The textbooks of the history of philosophy describe with greater or less fulness the processes which led, after Hegel's death, to the dissolution of his school. These processes are not without their great importance when considered with reference to the general history of European civilization in the nineteenth century. Unfortunately, however, the fortunes of the Hegelian "school" are less enlightening than we could wish concerning the genuine merit either of Hegel's own doctrine or of idealism in general. The questions that Kant had raised, and that the intermediate idealistic systems had after all quite inadequately developed, were not thoroughly considered upon their merits in the course of the controversies that attended the divisions and the final dissolution of the Hegelian school. There is no disrespect to German scholarship involved in asserting that the fortunes of university controversies in Germany are seldom wholly determined by an absolutely just and thoroughgoing consideration of the merits of the issues which form the topic of such controversies. So soon as a school has been formed, and so soon, therefore, as the fortunes of the members of such a school are bound up with their success or failure in getting or in keeping the attention of the academic public, extraneous motives are introduced into the life of scholarship. The influence of a school may give for a time undue weight to the published words of its members. The consciousness that there is a school sometimes leads for a while to an unprofitable devotion to merely external forms of expression, such as have come to characterize the members of the school. When opposition arises and begins to be successful, it leads only too frequently not only to a rejection of the current formulas of the school which is opposed but to a tendency to believe that if one abandons the formulas, one may henceforth simply neglect the thoughts that lay behind them. Hardly anything in fact is more injurious to the life of scholarship in general, and especially of philosophy, than the too strict and definite organization of schools of investigation. The life of academic scholarship depends upon individual liberty. And above all does the life of philosophy demand the initiative of the individual teacher as well as that of the individual pupil. A philosophy merely accepted from another man and not thought out for one's self is as dead as a mere catalogue of possible opinions. Philosophical formulas merely repeated upon the credit of a master's authority lose the very meaning which made the master authoritative. The inevitable result of the temporary triumph of an apparently closed school of university teachers of philosophy, who undertake to be the disciples of a given master, leads to the devitalizing of the master's thought, and to a revulsion, in the end, of opinion. People with any originality and independence of life pass on to new interests. The school becomes not an organization but a mere specimen preserved as in a museum, a relic of what was formerly alive. That was what happened before very long to so much of the Hegelian school as undertook to remain true to the mere tradition of the master.

Furthermore, new issues came to occupy the public mind as the nineteenth century proceeded. Theological issues due in part to the new development in the history of religion, new scientific discoveries occurring all over the field of empirical research, new political interests, which brought men out of sympathy with the political conservatism of Hegel's later years—all these motives combined to make men feel that Hegel's methods, identified as they were in most men's minds with Hegel's complex and ill-understood technical vocabulary, and so with the mere formalism of the system, were inadequate to cope with the new needs. Hegel's own confidence of tone, his air of superiority, his far too manifest willingness to regard his own formulations as final, led to a natural revolt. And because Hegel's form of idealism had been the most definite and for a while the most successful, the public mind confused its revised estimate of the value of Hegel's formulas with a supposed discovery of the inadequacy of the entire result of the early post-Kantian idealism. Men became increasingly suspicious of philosophical formulation, increasingly hopeless of success in the construction of philosophical systems, and increasingly devoted, for several decades after 1830, to special researches in the rapidly advancing and various branches of minute scholarship on the one hand, and of natural science on the other.

Yet the influence of early idealism has indeed never

passed away from European thought. As we saw in our opening discussion, this influence has been Protean, and has appeared in the most various places. So far as technical philosophizing is concerned, the most definite influence to which later thought has been subjected, is the influence of a more or less modified Kantianism. And as thus modified, the Kantian doctrine has always tended to express itself in the form of what one might call an empirical idealism,—an idealism of which the movement called "pragmatism" or "humanism," in this country and in England, is a more or less definite instance. An empirical idealism accepts, in the first place, so much of Kant's original doctrine as insisted that our knowledge is limited to phenomena. It then, in general, recognizes that our interpretations of phenomena involve no merely passive acceptance and report of data whose origin is wholly external to ourselves and indifferent to the interests of our own intelligence. At the very least our knowledge of the world involves, and in part depends upon, our own way of reacting to the world. A reality which has nothing to do with the life of our own intelligence, and which is so external to us as to be entirely independent of whether we know it or not, is indeed, from the point of view of such an empirical idealism, meaningless and to be neglected. To say that experience is our guide, is to admit with Kant that the conditions which determine the unity and the connectedness of our own experience are conditions in terms of which we are obliged to interpret reality; so that what we call real is inevitably adjusted in some sense to the demands of our intelligence. The recognition of this general thought appears in the most manifold shapes in modern discussion. Positivists and radical empiricists, formulators of new religious doctrine and investigators of the logic of science, evolutionists and various modern types of mystics, are thus found in often decidedly unconscious agreement which lies beneath their most marked differences. This agreement relates to the fact that our world is not merely given to us from without but is interpreted from within, so that what we mean by reality is always more or less idealized by us, that is, interpreted in terms of our own reason, even when we are ourselves most resolved to be passive and to accept the hard facts as we find them. Side by side with the question of Locke, "What are we men fitted to know?" philosophy must always face the question, "What is fit to be known?" And in terms of the latter question every theory of reality, however tentative, however skeptical, however radically empiristic it tries to be, will always more or less consciously be determined. What I regard as the permanent triumph, not of any one idealistic system, but of the idealistic spirit in the history of human thought, is indicated whenever a man tries to tell you what his view about the real world which our sciences study and our industrial arts endeavor to conquer, seems to him to be. One who states his view may believe that he is a hard and fast realist. But in modern times one of the reasons upon which he is likely to insist, will be one upon which President G. Stanley Hall has insisted in his book on *Adolescence*. This reason will be that a faith in the real world, as being something independent of the minds of us fallible mortals, is the only wholesome doctrine, the only corrective of the intellectual excesses of youth, the only safeguard against visionary and possibly morbid waywardness. But whoever expresses himself thus announces an explicitly idealistic theory, since he defines the nature of reality in terms of his ideal of wholesomeness. President Hall has his idea of what a healthy youth ought to be. This ideal demands that a youth, or anybody who teaches philosophy to the youth, should view the world in a certain way. This shows that the view in question is true. Hence, in substance, the real world is such as to embody the ideals of President G. Stanley Hall. These are robust ideals unquestionably; but the man who interprets his world in terms of them is a philosophical idealist, although it is part of his creed that he must not admit this fact even to himself. Such is a characteristic instance of the ways in which the idealistic tendency appears in modern thought. It has a character similar to that which Hegel in the *Phaenomenologie* attributed to the eighteenth-century Enlightenment. Modern idealism, like that former rationalism, is a sort of universal and often secret infection. Whoever contends against it shows that he is already its victim. He is undertaking to determine by his own rational ideals what the real world genuinely is, that is, how it ought to be conceived. By virtue of his very reasoning he confesses that the question, ''How ought I to conceive the real?'' is logically prior to the question, ''What is the real itself?'' And as a recent German writer, Professor Rickert, has pointed out, the *ought* is prior in nature to the real, or the proposition: ''I ought to think thus,'' is prior to the proposition: ''This is so.'' This whole view of the problem of reality is one which is characteristic of idealism.

This is why the idealistic movement in later European thought, although frequently suppressed, although often deliberately ignored, has been as constant as the movement of a great river beneath masses of winter ice. Every now and then the ice breaks or melts, and the idealistic tendency comes to the light of consciousness. It is irrepressible, because it is human. It is true, because truth itself is inevitably an ideal, which cannot possibly be expressed except in ideal terms. One who has become aware of this universal significance of the idealistic tendency, becomes indifferent to that general hostility towards either philosophy or idealism which is so often expressed by the unreflective. Let anybody tell you why he refuses to interpret his world in idealistic terms and he at once confesses his latent idealism; for he can express himself only by defining his ideal of scientific method, or by confessing his practical attitude towards the universe. In either case he defines his real world in terms of his ideal. His account may be in itself adequate or inadequate; in any case he is an idealist. Let him say, as is most customary, that he rejects all a priori ideas of things, because experience is his only guide, and you have only to ask him what he means by experience to discover that he accepts as belonging to the range of human experience a vast collection of data which he himself has never personally experienced and never hopes to experience. For however carefully I observe, my observations are but a fragment of that experience of mankind in terms of which I am constantly interpreting my own personal experience. Not only is the experience of mankind indefinitely wider than this one man's experience, but the experience of mankind is also something that, in its totality or in any of its larger connections, is never present in the experience of any one man, whoever he may be. How then does any one of us know what human experience, on the whole, verifies or proves? I answer, "We accept as human experience what certain social tests require us to regard as validly reported, as significantly related to our own observation, as such that it is reasonable to view this as experience, although we ourselves do not directly verify the fact that it is experience. Our conception of human experience is, therefore, itself no directly verifiable concept. It is determined by certain ideal motives which common sense defines in terms of reasonableness, and which the most exact scientific method can never define in other than distinctly ideal terms. It meets the need of our thinking processes to accept as empirical fact a great deal that we do not ourselves verify but believe other men to have verified." What William James calls "the sentiment of rationality" guides every such acceptance of other men's experience. The most radical empiricism is, therefore, full of idealistic motives. What it accepts as the verdict of experience is accepted in accordance with the demands of a certain sentiment of rationality, whose validity we have from moment to moment to accept on the ground that it would be unreasonable, that it would run counter to our ideal of truthfulness, not to accept this validity. I am of course not arguing that whatever phase a given individual chooses as his guide from moment to moment is a valid guide. I am merely pointing out that no criticism of the faith that customarily guides men can reduce it to a purely empirical test; because no empirical test can be applied unless we use some form of faith, some sentiment of rationality, in terms of which we define and accept something or other as constituting the experience of mankind. Philosophy must indeed criticize as thoroughly as it is able the various tests that we actually use, the various faiths upon which men act, the Protean forms of the sentiment of rationality. What I insist upon is that such a criticism must itself in the long run be guided by a conscious rational ideal, which when it becomes conscious must appear as the ideal of our own intelligence, of the self that speaks through us, of the reason of which we are the embodiment. Hence whoever appeals to experience, or to any other test regarding what is real, inevitably interprets the world, whether of external reality or of human experience, in terms of the demands which his own rational consciousness formulates. In other words, whoever has a world at all has it as the expression of ideal demands which his intelligent self when it comes to consciousness formulates as its own.

For my part, therefore, I am fond of hearing men formulate a condemnation of the principles of idealism. The more definitely they formulate their condemnation, the more explicitly do they define their world as the expression of their own ideal regarding the way in which it is rational to think the world. Their voice is the voice of idealism, however much they may try to disguise it. They look straight outward; and thereupon, as it were, deny that they have any eyes, because they see no such objects about them. They assert that the world is in essence independent of the motives which lead them to formulate their assertions; but when asked why their assertions are true can only name again these motives. They say, "This is my thought." Yet they deny that reality is in any wise essentially related to the expression of thought. They possess then, in the concrete, the spirit of idealism. I welcome them as exponents of this spirit. They simply lack self-consciousness as to what their position is. And this lack is, after all, very much their own affair.

So far I have pointed out only the most general way in which an idealistic tendency finds its place in recent thought. The idealistic character of recent philosophy will be present to consciousness in so far as influences, amongst which Kant's *Critique of Pure Reason* is in many ways the most prominent, have made us apt to reflect upon the presuppositions of every inquiry, and upon the way in which every formulation of the results of thought, however empirical in its detail, must receive its form from the ideal interests which constitute the essential character of our own reason, and which also lie at the basis of our conduct. Such a general idealism remains, so far, characteristic of the spirit of modern thought rather than constitutive of any one system of philosophy. As soon as one attempts to formulate this idealistic spirit in any series of propositions about the world of our experience and about its interpretation in terms of the rational ideals which guide our thinking and our conduct, great opportunities arise for a divergence of opinions regarding the constitution of this world, and for different ways of emphasis regarding the relative importance of the various interests by which our estimate of the world is determined. A philosophy is inevitably the expression of a mental attitude which one assumes towards life and towards the universe. This attitude is at once theoretical and practical—theoretical because it undertakes to define opinions concerning the nature of things, and practical because every effort to define opinions is essentially an expression of one's interest in the universe, and so of one's ideals of conduct. But every such attitude is inevitably colored by one's individuality. It is a person who interprets things. This person inevitably emphasizes some aspect of the world which nobody else emphasizes in the same way, and undertakes activities which are in some respects the activities of no other person. Now if truth is ideally significant, and if ideals are always centered about individual persons, it will always be impossible to formulate philosophical doctrines without leaving open the opportunity for a variety of individual formulation. This does not mean that the truth is at the mercy of private caprice, or that any man is his own measure of all things, without reference to other men. It *does* mean that the whole of philosophy can only exist in an essentially social form, as the synthesis of many—yes, ideally speaking, of an infinite number—of individual and personal points of view, whose diversity will be due to the fact that the truth must mirror various aspects of its constitution in various ways in the diverse individuals. The world, in other words, interprets itself through us, that is, through whatever rational individuals there are. The interpretations cannot be, ought not to be, monotonously uniform. If they were, they would simply be abstractions, and so would be monotonously inadequate and false. Inadequate our individual interpretations indeed always remain. But they need not be monotonously inadequate. They must properly supplement one another.

The aim of philosophy is, then, the synthesis of these individual varieties of interpretation. Since synthesis depends first upon mutual understanding, and then upon mutual correction of inadequacy, our instrument as we aim towards synthesis must involve a constant effort to find what is common to various experiences, to various individual interpretations, to various thoughtful processes. Our empirical sciences depend essentially upon confirming one man's experiences by the experiences of other men; and therefore these sciences recognize as objective fact only what can be verified in common by various observers. Similiarly our logical and ethical inquiries are concerned, although in another way than the one followed in empirical science, with the effort to define common and universal categories and laws which express the will of all men. But when the best has been done thus to discover the common features of our various experiences and ideals, a most significant aspect of the universe will have been inevitably omitted in every such investigation. And this will be precisely the aspect of individuality in the universe. If the world is essentially a life of will and of thought coming to an individual consciousness of itself in and through various personalities whose social unity rests upon their very variety, the work of discovering the truth can never exhaustively be reduced to the work of finding out what these various personalities find or will merely in common. They all in common mean, intend, experience, and think the universe. They are all, therefore, as Leibnitz said, mirrors of the universe. But since the universe is, from this point of view, just the system of living mirrors itself, what is common to the various world-pictures is never the whole truth. Hence it is of the nature of a philosophy always to be in presence of problems which forbid a final systematic formulation from the point of view of the individual philosopher, just because these problems are soluble only from the point of view of other individuals. Philosophy, needing especially, as it does, to take account of the variety of individual points of view rather than of common features, is, therefore, much less able than are the empiri-

cal sciences to define a settled result upon which further
investigation may be based. When a length is measured,
one is looking for what is common to various individual
experiences regarding this length. That common element
may be approximately determined once for all. And
upon that result a scientific theory of physical facts may
depend for further progress. A philosophy, however, is
essentially concerned with an unity of truth which can
only be expressed through the variety of individual
points of view. Hence it does not define an abstract common feature of various experiences as a fact upon which
further research is to be founded merely by means of an
accretion of further facts of the same sort.

Thus everything in philosophy is properly subject to
re-interpretation from new individual points of view.
No sincere individual point of view is absolutely erroneous, for every such interpretation is a portion of the interpretation which the universe gives to itself through
the variety of individuals. On the other hand, every finite
individual's account of the world is subject to re-interpretation and in the progress of thinking will doubtless
become, so to speak, absorbed in higher syntheses. At any
point in time the returns, so far as truth is concerned, are
not all in. For countless individual interpretations have
not yet been made, or are not now in synthesis. Hence
philosophy is peculiarly subject to the reproach of being
unfinished and unstable. But people do not reproach life
with instability in the case where it furnishes us with
novelty and with the opportunity for significant progress. Truth is not merely capricious and subjective because new individual expressions are needed to supplement every finite interpretation. It is the value and not
the defect of philosophy that it proceeds not by mere

accumulation of settled discoveries, but by a constant re-interpretation of the meaning of life.*

III.

When I now speak, therefore, of the unsettled problems of idealism, I do so not in a spirit of mere skepticism, and not with the intent of merely confessing ignorance, and still less with a disposition to assert in a dogmatic way just how I suppose these problems ought to be settled. I want rather to suggest some of the conditions upon which, as I suppose, our interpretation of these problems and of their relation to life, will be based.

The unsettled problems of which I speak are of a nature which the foregoing discussion has already indicated. The first problem which the various forms of idealistic doctrine have endeavored to consider is one that in the later idealism, since Hegel's death, became especially noticeable, although we have found Hegel dealing with it. It is the problem of the relation between the rational and the irrational features of reality. The world of our experience becomes a rational realm to us in so far as we can interpret it in terms of ideas that adequately express our own conscious purpose. Thus, in so far as I can count objects, and can operate with numbers which correspond to the results of such counting, the facts with which I deal possess for me what might be called the numerical type of reasonableness. In so far as I can measure phenomena and get exact results, and in so far as in terms of the results of former measurements I can predict the results of future measurements, I deal with a world of

---

* In this whole discussion are foreshadowed some elements of the later theory of interpretation as expounded in *The Problem of Christianity.*—ED.

experience—a world of phenomena—which possesses quantitative reasonableness. In so far as I can get control of phenomena, as for instance our industrial arts get a very vast and socially significant control of the phenomena of human experience, so that we can define in advance what we want, and by doing a definite piece of work can attain the required results, our world possesses what may be called practical reasonableness. If we pass directly to the social realm, individual men show themselves as reasonable in so far as they can learn to live and work together, not destroying or suppressing their individual varieties, but winning essential harmony even in and through these varieties. Now it is perfectly plain that for the civilized man a considerable portion of this world of experience has become a rational world. On the other hand, it is equally obvious that we are constantly in presence of what so far appears to us as an irrational aspect of our experience. There are phenomena which we cannot adequately describe and predict in terms of our processes of numbering or of measuring. There are countless phenomena, such as storms and earthquakes and diseases and criminal propensities, which we cannot as yet control. Social life is a constant contention with the unreasonable forces which tend toward social anarchy. The individuality of every man appears at once as the most reasonable and as the most unreasonable feature about him—the most reasonable because what we most value in humanity, what love most emphasizes, what our social longing most idealizes, what our rational passion of liberty most insists upon is the individual human being, so that whatever gives our reasonable life its value, its friends to love, its task to perform is something individual. Yet, on the other hand, the individuality of everybody appears also as the unreasonable aspect of human nature in so far as individuality means whim, caprice, waywardness, oddity, eccentricity—in brief, whatever about any human being involves rebellion against order and intrusion upon the will of one's fellows. Thus our world of experience is a synthesis of what appear to us at present rational and irrational features. The history of society, and in particular of religion, of science, and of philosophy, appears to us as a warfare of reason and unreason. The world is, then, at least in appearance irrational in so far as it refuses at any moment to express our meaning, to embody the categories of our thought, to realize the ideals of our conduct, to permit the unity of consciousness to come into synthesis with the brute facts of sense and of emotion. Now what a realistic philosophy would interpret as the contrast between independent facts and our subjective ideas, an idealistic philosophy must conceive as the contrast between the rational and the irrational elements or aspects of experience and of life.

In the history of idealism in the nineteenth century the conflict between rationalism and irrationalism appeared as the principal motive for the abandonment of systems such as Hegel's, and for the tendency to attempt constantly new formulations of the idealistic conception of the universe. Hegel, especially as interpreted by the formalists of his own school, appeared to the generation which followed his death as an extreme rationalist who regarded the world as through and through the expression of rational ideals which the philosopher could formulate. The idealistic opposition to Hegel later received its classical representation in the doctrine of Schopenhauer. Schopenhauer, whose doctrine did not become influential until after 1850, is the classical irrationalist of the rationalistic movement. For him, the universe has a two-fold aspect. It is the world as idea, that is, the world as consciousness defines and observes it. In so far, it is a world subject to the categories, or again on its highest level, it is the world as the artist views and portrays it. Thus, it is either a world subject to law, or a world instinct with beautiful types of life. So far, then, it is the world of reason, or at least of what we may venture to call ideally significant unity. But on the other hand, the world possesses quite a different aspect. It is the world of the will. The will is the principle of irrational desire, of unrest, of brute fact, of conflict. The world as will is always deeper than the world as idea. The world as idea is the world of forms, intellectual or artistic—the world as known to the rational inquirer, or to the contemplative artist. But the world as will is the material aspect of things, which appears in our experience as brute fact, as mere data, as the restless incompleteness of every phase of life. The world as will is essentially bad, base, unideal, incomprehensible, unfathomable. The world as idea is the world of the apparition of this incomprehensible principle in forms which can either be understood or contemplated, but which can thus be understood or contemplated only in their relative, their imperfect, or their merely phenomenal aspect. No idealism can, therefore, hope to see the world as a rational whole. It is not a rational whole. Consciousness is merely a flickering light that shows to us in a more or less definite form the beautiful surface of the waste ocean of the unconscious and irrational will.

That this view expresses an aspect which experience constantly forces upon our attention, has just been pointed out. Schopenhauer was not alone in defining the outcome of idealism in such terms. Schelling, in his later period of thought from 1809, when he published an essay on the nature of free will to the close of his career, emphasized the presence of an irrational principle in the universe to which human caprice and the brute facts of experience are due. In later idealism, von Hartmann is a notable example of one who conceives the nature of things in terms of a fundamental irrationalism. The age of the doctrine of evolution, emphasizing as it has done the struggle for existence, has given weight to the considerations upon which Schopenhauer and von Hartmann have insisted.

IV.

Closely connected with considerations of this type are those which must have been near to your minds as you followed my sketch of the Hegelican doctrine. Is the idealistic philosopher able to define in any sense a priori the constitution which things must have? Or is he, like the student of the special sciences, confined to interpreting the results of human experience? Hegel was regarded by his contemporaries and successors as an extravagant apriorist, who endeavored to deduce the facts of nature and of history out of his own inner consciousness. In truth, Hegel made a sharp distinction between our learning by experience as we do learn what occurs and what has occurred, and our interpreting, in the light of the categories of our philosophy, the total meaning of this result of experience. Hegel recognized that we learn of our world through experience, and that unless something is first present in experience and in life, it is useless for philosophy to try to interpret what this something means. But he had, on the other hand, an unquestionably extravagant disposition to regard his philosophical interpretation of the meaning of experience as actually adequate to the whole of it. Meanwhile, the form of the philosophical interpretation must, so he held, be internally rational, that is, such as to make the connections clear to the philosopher as he proceeds. But this internal form of the philosophical system will in so far be a priori. Philosophy will thus be a reconstruction of experience in terms which the inner necessity of things determines. Hegel's extravagant confidence was that such an interpretation had actually been accomplished by his philosophy. He did not suppose that if we had never been enlightened by experience we could deduce a priori the nature of the world. But he did suppose that experience had at last attained a point of view from which it is possible to reconstruct, by an a priori method, precisely so much of the meaning of experience as is in fact rational.

However, as we have already seen, Hegel himself recognized a certain truth in irrationalism. It was an essential feature of his dialectical method that he should recognize such a truth. Reason is for him an active process. It therefore involves the aspect which Schopenhauer emphasized as the will. For Hegel as for Schopenhauer, the life of the will is essentially a life of contest. It is necessary that the will should be in conflict with its own opponent. But the opponent of the will is at any stage the irrational, the undesired, the unintended, the apparently brutal fact over which the will at each stage has to win its way by an act of conquest. Hence the difference between Hegel and Schopenhauer is essentially this: Hegel insists upon the thesis that it is rational for the reason, being as it is both practical and theoretical, to meet and to conquer an irrational element in its experience. Or again, there is an a priori necessity that we should constantly meet in our finite experience with contents which we cannot as yet deduce a priori. To express it otherwise, there is an a priori necessity that the a priori demands of the reason should always find over against them an empirical element of brute fact which cannot be deduced a priori. In still other words, Hegel recognizes an element of objective chance in the nature of things. It belongs to the dialectic of his system to do so. In this way Hegel is indeed an apriorist. He is an extravagant apriorist, in so far as he is confident of the finality of his own interpretation of nature and of life, and in so far as he actually neglects a great number of facts upon which experience has taught the rest of us to lay great stress. But Hegel has a place for empiricism, and a place for the irrational in his system.

It belongs to the spirit of the time that the later idealism should emphasize, as every reasonable idealist now does, the constant claims of experience upon the philosopher. To recognize this is simply to point out that no individual interpretation can be final. On the other hand, every idealist must emphasize the fact that we cannot and do not move a step in our thinking without using the a priori, that is, without appealing to that which for internal reasons we consciously regard as the rationally thoughtful way of interpreting the present facts of experience. I now recognize and acknowledge the existence of your minds as relatively external to my own mind. But this recognition, this acknowledgment, is not now for me a mere acceptance of a brute fact of sense. For your experience is just now no experience of mine. My acknowledgment that you are there in my world is an interpretation. And for this interpretation I can give no reasons which are not in part a priori, reasons definable in terms of an internal necessity which my consciousness makes manifest to itself in its own way. Similarly, my own past and my own future, the very existence of any world beyond the present, the assertion of any fact in heaven or in earth, depends indeed in part upon the momentary pressure of experience, but equally upon an internally necessary and a priori demand of reason.

V.

I have now briefly reviewed two great problems of recent idealism, that of the relation of the rational to the irrational aspect of experience, and that of the relation of empiricism and the acceptance of truth as a priori, that is, as internally necessary. No single formulation of an answer to either of these problems will ever prove, within the range of our human experience, to be adequate. For each problem will constantly present itself in new aspects as life and as individuality diversify. But already I have indicated the spirit in which I think we must always meet these problems. As a fact, both problems involve a distinction of aspect. We must not confound these aspects. Yet we must not divide the substance of life into two different and ultimate sorts of truth or reality in order to be just to the diversity of aspect.

First, as to the problem of the a priori. The whole world is indeed known to me by experience, precisely in so far as experience restlessly awakens me to the fact that there is something still before me to acknowledge and something still before me to do. But the whole world is inevitably defined by me at any instant a priori, in so far as my present experience is meaningless except with reference to facts which I regard as past or as future, or as yonder in time or in space, as matters of possible experience, not just now verifiable, as matters belonging to other individual lives than mine, as contents finding their place in a certain conceived order of things. The only warrant for such acknowledgment of what is not given must be found by me in a priori terms, and must be ultimately warranted by the consideration that unless I acknowledge a realm of facts not now verified by me, I simply contradict myself and reduce my experience to a meaningless chaos. From this point of view, your laboratory man, or your field naturalist, or your business man in the market place or your man of common sense, or even your light-hearted child at play, is as much an apriorist as the philosopher. For all these dwell in a world that is to them no mere datum, but a construction. This is the eternal truth of Kant's deduction of the categories. This is the true sense in which the universe is interpreted by everybody as the expression of the more or less conscious demand of the rational self. In this respect the world is always a conceptual construct, in other words, a world known a priori. The ultimate warrant for such an interpretation is always the principle of contradiction, the principle of inner necessity. For St. Augustine long ago formulated the matter: If I assert that there is no truth, I assert that it is true that there is no truth, and consequently contradict myself. But my truth is always my interpretation of my situation, and is thus in its form a priori, although its matter is determined by whatever feelings, images, sensations and interests I chance to find uppermost at any moment of my individual life. We are all therefore both empiricists and apriorists. And whenever you find a man condemning in a sweeping way all a priori construction as inadequate to discover the constitution of the hard and fast realm of facts, you will always find upon looking closer that what he then means by his hard and fast world of facts is known to him just then in terms of a conceptual construction which he then and there acknowledges upon a priori grounds. I am very willing, then, to hear people condemn the a priori; for I notice that they do so upon a priori grounds.

A closely analogous consideration must guide our attitude towards the other problem, that of the relation between the rational and the irrational aspects of the world. The fact, for instance, that my friend is dead, and that I shall never see him in this world again, or that popular tumult rages in Russia in irrational madness, may be to my mind an opaque and in so far an irrational fact. Yet I always acknowledge that fact, save from this moment outward, as something whose reality is acknowledged by me upon rational, that is, internally necessary grounds. My world of fact is to me, therefore, at once rational and irrational. It at once expresses my meaning, fulfils my rational demands, and disappoints me, limits me, forces upon me what I do not now comprehend. But I further observe, that my acknowledgment of the irrationality of a fact is always an instance of the inadequacy of my comprehension of that fact. My conflict with the fact is at the same time a conflict with the imperfection of my own insight. There are facts which at first appear to me irrational, such as the puzzling conditions to which I must conform when I learn the rudiments of a new art. Yet when I learn the art, I learn to control and thus to rationalize the very facts that I also

254

learn to acknowledge as real. When one learns to ride a bicycle, there are moments, perhaps days, when nothing appears so irrational as the physical behavior of this unaccustomed object, which falls over when you move with the intention of keeping it upright, and runs towards what you most try to avoid. Later on, through conflict, this unreasonableness of the object becomes transformed into its controllable trustworthiness of lawful behavior. Facts may, therefore, be relatively irrational, their irrationality meaning simply my imperfect insight into my world, my imperfect possession of my own principles of conduct. The problem of irrationality, like the problem of evil, which is an instance of the problem of irrationality, always comes to us so joined with the problem of our own inadequacy of knowledge that we can never tell how far a supplementing of our insight will lead us to an acknowledgment of the reasonableness of what we first find unreasonable. But you may very rightly say that thus the problem of the unreasonable becomes transferred to ourselves, and the question why we are so finite, so ignorant, and so unreasonable still remains insoluble. But here appears a consideration which our historical sketch has especially prepared us, in this closing summary, to estimate.

The dialectical method, as we remember, has especially insisted upon the fact that the practical life of the spirit depends upon developing and overcoming opposition. One may regard this doctrine of the older idealists either as an empirical generalization from historical and psychological phenomena, or as an a priori rational principle. For reasons which I have indiciated in the foregoing, I myself regard it as possessing equally both of these characters. The value of antithesis and of conflict is verifiable empirically in very numerous instances. Not only does the will actually seek conflict, as both Hegel and Schopenhauer emphasize; but despite Schopenhauer's insistence that such voluntary conflict belongs to the merely irrational side of the will, we must maintain with Hegel that extremely lofty rational interest both of the will and of the whole spiritual nature are such as to demand the presence of conflicting motives and even of essentially tragic contests in all the higher spiritual life. The truth, whatever it is, is certainly not expressible in merely abstract, or in merely harmonious terms. If it is the truth of life, i.e., if the truth is a living and not a merely bloodless realm of abstract categories, then the truth must involve issues, struggles, conquests, and conquests over aspects of life that, when viewed in their abstraction, are distinctly evil and irrational. If once this principle, which Hegel's *Phaenomenologie* so richly illustrates, is admitted as essentially valid, then it is surely difficult to estimate the extent to which the existence of apparently irrational elements and facts can exist in the world not merely as forming an exception to the reasonableness of things, but as facts which seen, as it were, from above, and in their genuine unity with all other facts, are actually essential to the unity of things and to the rationality of the universe. From this point of view it seems at least possible to say that the union of rational and irrational or evil facts in the universe at large is itself, when the universe is taken in its wholeness, an essentially rational union, so that the evils are there to be conquered simply because otherwise the triumphant reasonableness, which from an absolute point of view is expressed in such conquest, would be impossible. Perhaps, then, just as all knowledge is empirical and all knowledge of significant facts is inevitably also a priori; so now we may say that the world is a rational whole, and yet any finite fact in it, if viewed in its isolation, if viewed with forgetfulness of its relation to the absolute point of view, may to any extent be evil and irrational. The narrow life may be base; yet through a conquest over this baseness the larger life with which this narrow life, as an expression, is bound up may be triumphantly rational.

VI.

The suggestion of any such thesis brings us to another question, the last which we have time to consider. Idealism has appeared in recent thought partly as pragmatism, insisting that all truth is practical, that is, is true by virtue of its practical relation to some finite need. For many thinkers, pragmatism is essentially opposed to an absolutism which suggests, or perhaps positively maintains, that the world in its wholeness has an absolute constitution in the light of which all finite truth must be interpreted. Now I myself am far from pretending to possess any peculiar revelation as to what the content of absolute truth may be. But I do maintain that a pragmatist to whom whatever is true, is true relatively, that is, with reference to some finite need or definition, is actually as much in need as I am of attributing to his world whatever constitution it actually possesses. Truth meets needs; truth is also true. Of these two propositions I conceive idealism to be constituted. If one attempts to define a world of merely relative truth, this world, as soon as you define it in its wholeness, becomes once more your absolute, your truth that is true. In acknowledging truth we are indeed meeting, or endeavoring to meet, a need which always expresses itself in finite form. But

257

this need can never be satisfied by the acknowledgment
of anything finite as the whole truth. For, as Hegel well
insisted, the finite is as such self-contradictory, dialectical, burdened with irrationality. It passes away. Meanwhile it struggles with its own contradictions, and will
not be content with acknowledging anything less than its
own fulfilment in an Absolute Life which is also an absolute truth. That many are not conscious of this need, I
agree. Most men have no great amount of consciousness
with regard to anything. But that all are discontent with
their finitude, is a matter of common experience. I interpret this as implying, and as inevitably implying, that
it is the truth that every finite life actually finds its fulfilment in an Absolute Life, in which we live and move
and have our being. I maintain, and have elsewhere at
length argued, that to attempt to deny this Absolute Life,
is simply to reaffirm it under some new form. That the
Absolute Life has to be conceived as the absolute union of
experience and of rational necessity, of freedom and of
law, of infinitude and finitude, of what we regard as irrational and of what we view as rational, I have elsewhere maintained at length. I am not here to preach my
own doctrine. But I may assert that personally I am both
a pragmatist and an absolutist, that I believe each of
these doctrines to involve the other, and that therefore
I regard them not only as reconcilable but as in truth
reconciled.

Herewith, in sketching these problems of later idealism I have also suggested what I take to be the present
position of idealistic doctrine. And herewith, in consequence, the wholly fragmentary and illustrative task of
these present lectures is completed. Something may have
been gained by these fragmentary discussions, if they

have suggested that idealistic philosophy is not merely a collection of eccentric opinions held by lonely students, but despite the eccentricity and the loneliness of many of the phases of its formulation, is not only in essential sympathy with the rational study of experience and with the practical ideals of life, but is at least unconsciously what I hope it will more and more consciously become, the expression of the very soul of our civilization. For we all not only gather but interpret experience. And to interpret experience is to regard facts as the fulfilment of rational ideals. And we all not only accept life but try to conquer its irrationality, and to idealize its finitude. So to act is essentially, whether we know it or not, to view the temporal as the symbol and the likeness of the eternal.

INDEX

Absolute, The, 54; social motives explaining its use, 55; concept of, Lecture III, *passim;* as problem for the post-Kantians, 71 ff.; in relation to theology, 75; as Schelling's "Identity" or "Indifference," 133; art as the apparition of, 134; nature of, in Hegel's *Phenomenology,* 167 ff.; Hegel's theory of, as evolutionary and non-temporal, 170; characteristics of, in contrast with finite self, 174 ff.; in terms of the religious consciousness, 209 ff.; in relation to Hegel's theory of truth, 215 ff.; as *Idee,* 221; as life and truth, 257 ff.

Adolescence, by Stanley Hall, 236.

"Animals, The Intellectual," in Hegel's *Phenomenology,* 196 ff.

Antigone, 203.

Antinomies, 56, 80, 154.

Antithetical Method. *See* Dialectical Method.

Aristotle, 46, 214.

Art, Schelling's interpretation of, 121, 134; Hegel's view of, 210, 229.

Attention, 26.

Baldwin, J. M., 127 f.

"*Beobachtende Vernunft,*" in Hegel's *Phenomenology,* 189.

Bradley, 2, 110.

Browning, 140 f.

Byron, 83 f.; quoted, 192 f.

Carlyle, 147.

Categories, 19 ff.; in relation to experience, 25, 32 ff., as a priori forms, 45; Aristotle's table of, 46; Hegelian, 174, 220 ff.

Causation, Kant's category of, 20.

Cervantes, 195.

Christian mystics, 75.

Conciousness, as stage in the *Phenomenology,* 150; its various *Gestalten,* 151 ff.; its meaning defined, 156; nature of absolute, in *Phenomenology,* 167 ff.; theoretical and practical stages of, 171 ff.; social character of absolute, 175; savage, illustrated, 176; of master and slave, 177 f.; of stoicism, 179; the unhappy, 180 ff.; analysis of pleasure-seeking, 190, of the romantic reformer, 193 f., of the knight-errant, 195, of the "intellectual animals," 195 ff.; social types of, 199 ff.; religious, 209 ff.

Contradiction, characteristic of dialectical method, 89; in self-consciousness, 90 ff.; in relation to truth, 94 ff.; not

261

INDEX

INDEX